Using Excel For

Karen Gutermuth
Virginia Military Institute

R. Carter Hill
Louisiana State University

UNDERGRADUATE
ECONOMETRICS
Second Edition

R. Carter Hill
Louisiana State University

William E. Griffiths
University of New England, Australia

George G. Judge
University of California at Berkeley

John Wiley & Sons, Inc.
New York • Chichester • Weinheim • Brisbane • Singapore • Toronto

To order books or for customer service call 1-800-CALL-WILEY (225-5945).

ISBN 0-471-41237-6

Printed in the United States of America

10 9 8 7 6 5 4 3 2 1

Printed and bound by Victor Graphics, Inc.

Contents

Preface

This book is a supplement to *Undergraduate Econometrics, 2nd Edition* by Carter Hill, Bill Griffiths and George Judge (Wiley, 2001), hereinafter *UE/2*. We show you how to perform the computations, step by step, in each chapter of that book using Microsoft Excel97 spreadsheet software. Consequently, this book will be useful to students taking econometrics, as well as their instructors, and others who wish to use Excel for econometric analysis. We have tried to include in this book all the material we would like our students to have at their fingertips as they read *UE/2* and work on the exercises therein.

We assume that the readers have a basic knowledge of Excel. If this is not the case there are many guides to the use of Excel97 that you will find at your local bookstore. Even so, we will start with some basics in the first chapter of this book.

Excel is not a statistics or econometrics software package. It is a very powerful spreadsheet program in which you can set up worksheets containing numbers and formulas, create graphs, and print the results. Output from Excel is easily incorporated into documents, simplifying report writing. Since it is not designed to do all types of statistical analysis, there will be some examples in *UE/2* that simply can not be done in Excel without extraordinary effort and programming skill.

In addition to supporting material for Excel users, the authors of *UE/2* provide support for the computer software packages SAS, SHAZAM and EViews. To find out more about these supplements visit their web site, **http://www.wiley.com/college/hill**. There the reader will also find all the data files used in *UE/2*, as well the Excel files mentioned in this volume, as well as other resources for students and instructors.

The chapters in this book parallel the chapters in *UE/2*. Thus if you seek help for the examples in Chapter 11 of the textbook, check Chapter 11 in this book.

We welcome comments about this book, and suggestions for improvements.

Karen Gutermuth
Department of Economics and Business
Virginia Military Institute
Lexington, VA 24450
GutermuthK@mail.vmi.edu

R. Carter Hill
Economics Department
Louisiana State University
Baton Rouge, LA 70803
eohill@lsu.edu

Excel Files Created in <u>Using Excel for Undergraduate Econometrics</u>, 2nd Edition

Chapter 3:   ch3.xls
Chapter 5:   citemplate.xls
               hyptesttemplate.xls
Chapter 6:   ch6.xls
Chapter 7:   hamburg.xls
Chapter 8:   hamburg.xls
               ftesttemplate.xls
               hamburg2.xls
               beerdemand.xls
               reset.xls
               manuf.xls
Chapter 9:   houseprice.xls
               GEWH_inv.xls
Chapter 10:   costs.xls
               pizza.xls
Chapter 11:   whitesterrs.xls
               proporhetero.xls
               GQtest.xls
               GQregs.xls
               wheat.xls
Chapter 12:   sugarcane.xls
Chapter 13:   MofM.xls
               savings.xls
Chapter 14:   truffles.xls
Chapter 15:   lagmodel.xls
Chapter 16:   cointer.xls
               dickeyfuller.xls
Chapter 17:   ftesttemplatech17.xls
               GEWH2.xls
               pool.xls
Chapter 18:   transport.xls
Chapter 19:   y_c.xls

Note: These files can be found at the textbook website, **http://www.wiley.com/college/hill**

Chapter 1 Introduction to Excel

In this introductory Chapter we cover the basics of importing data into Excel, saving a worksheet, and printing a worksheet.

1.1 Importing Data Into Excel

The data files provided by the authors of *UE/2* are ASCII, or text, files. In these files the data variables are in columns and the observations on those variables are in rows. A data file may have variable names in the first row.

The first task you face is to bring the data values into Excel, a step called *importing data*, for analysis. Excel has an "Import Wizard" to help with the process. Once we have it in Excel we can save the data as an Excel file, with an *.xls* extension. When the saved file is opened again at a later date, the data will immediately be placed in rows and columns correctly.

To illustrate, let us import the data found in Table 1.1 of Chapter 1 in *UE/2*. We will assume that you have the textbook data files in the folder **c:\datafiles**. First, open a new worksheet,

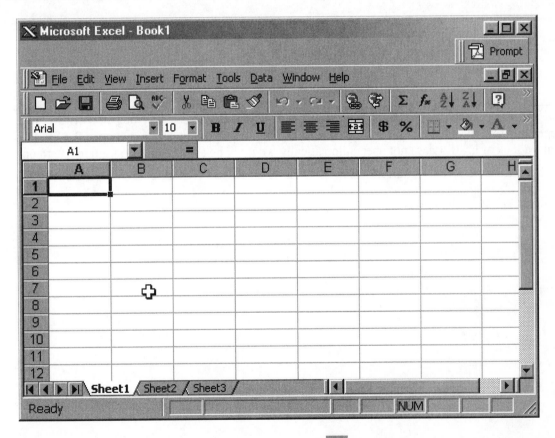

- From Excel, choose File/Open (or click on the Open icon). In the dialog box, locate the folder **datafiles** on the **c:** drive.

1

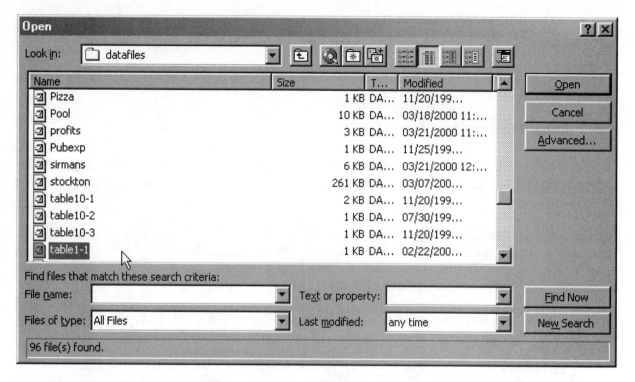

- Choose the file "*table1-1.dat*" which appears as the icon

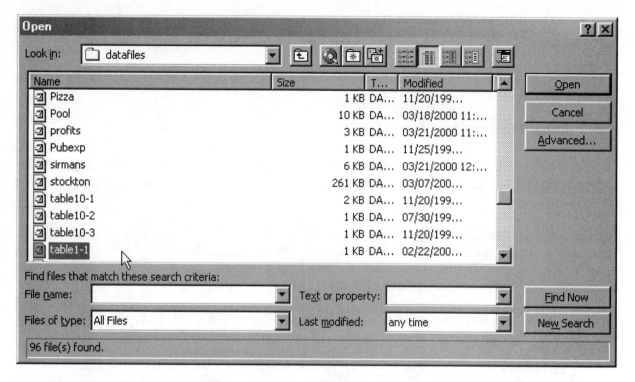 table1-1

Hint: The little symbol next to the name *table1-1* is the icon for Microsoft's Notepad software, which can open any text file. If you double click on *table1-1* in Windows Explorer it will open the file so you can take a look at it. If it does not open automatically, you will be asked what program to use to open this file. Scroll down the list until you find Notepad and select it.

The Import Wizard will appear.

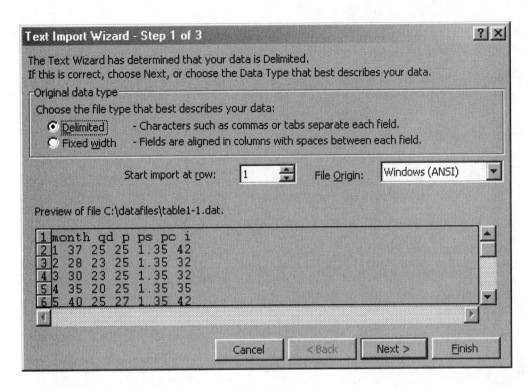

Note the Next and Back buttons. If you make a mistake in your choices of options, you can always go back to the previous screen and start over.

- Click on **Next**. Click in the box indicating that spaces are delimiters. Lines then appear dividing the cells into the proper variables. *Table1-1.dat* and **all the files provided for *UE/2* are space delimited**.

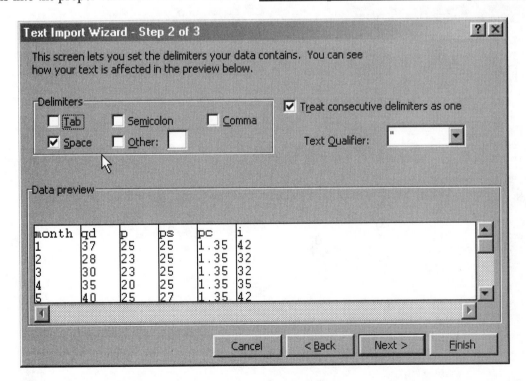

- Click **Next**. This window will allow you to set particular formats for each variable. Usually, the default format, which Excel calls **General**, will be suitable.

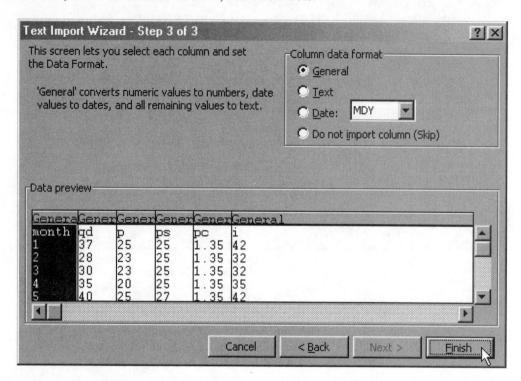

- When done, click **Finish**. Your data will appear (hopefully, correctly) in an Excel worksheet.

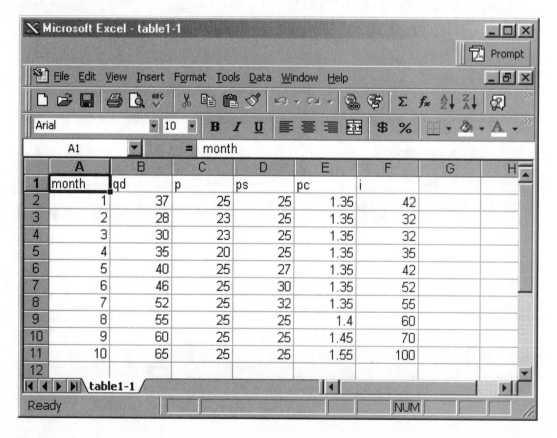

- Now we must save this worksheet so that we can use it at some future point without having to go through the data importation process. Click on the "**Save**" icon on the toolbar.

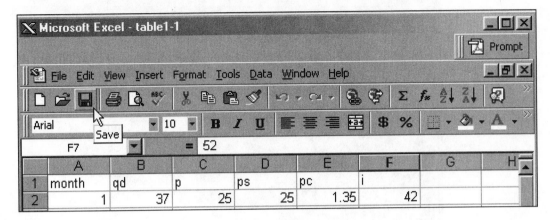

- Name the worksheet with a name that will mean something to you a month from now when you are looking for the file. We assume that you will save all your files in a folder **c:\Econometrics**. This file we save as **table1-1.xls**.

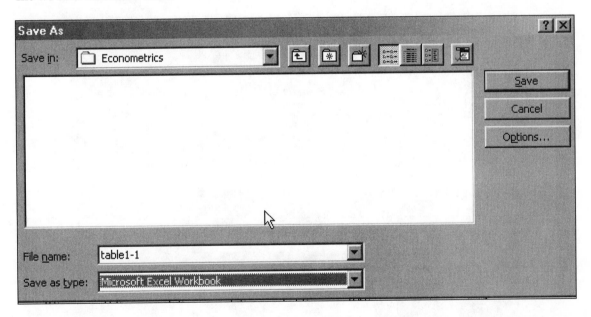

- Click **Save**. Now, when you open Excel again, and look in the folder **c:\Econometrics** you will find **table1-1.xls** ready for use.

1.2   Printing a Worksheet

- To print a worksheet, first click on **File/Page Setup**.

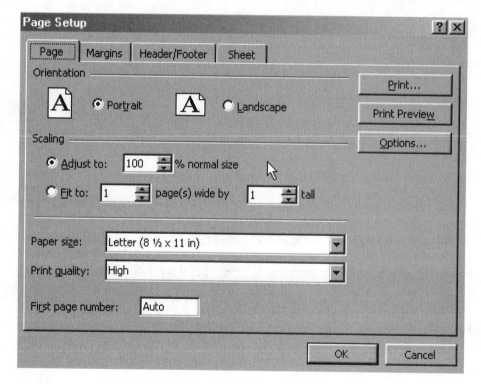

There you can choose the page layout, either **Portrait** or **Landscape**, and adjust the size. The **Print Preview** allows you to see what will be printed before actually doing so, which saves time and paper.

- Click on **File/Print** to open the print dialog window.

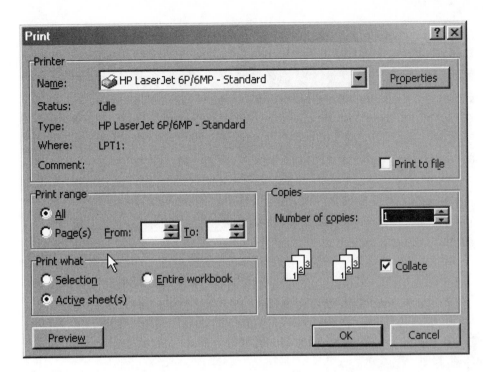

In the **Print** dialog box, make sure the printer is correctly specified. Here you can specify **Print range**, and **Print what**.

Alternatively, if the **Print Preview** was satisfactory, click on the printer icon on the main toolbar.

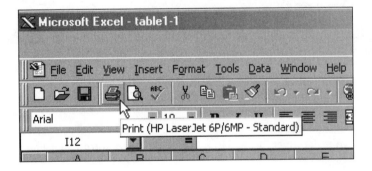

1.3   Copying to a Document

For report writing it is sometimes convenient to copy data from Excel into a word processor.
- Select the data you wish to copy by holding down the left mouse button. Drag it across the desired area of the worksheet. The selected cells will darken.

	A	B	C	D	E	F	G
1	month	qd	p	ps	pc	i	
2	1	37	25	25	1.35	42	
3	2	28	23	25	1.35	32	
4	3	30	23	25	1.35	32	
5	4	35	20	25	1.35	35	
6	5	40	25	27	1.35	42	
7	6	46	25	30	1.35	52	
8	7	52	25	32	1.35	55	
9	8	55	25	25	1.4	60	
10	9	60	25	25	1.45	70	
11	10	65	25	25	1.55	100	
12							

- On the main toolbar, click the **Copy** icon, or use the keystroke **Ctrl+C**.

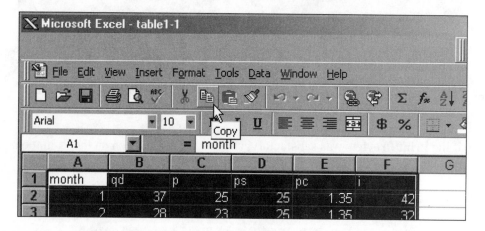

When you do so the border around the darkened cells will begin rotating.

- Open a new document, and click on the "paste" icon, , or use the keystroke **Ctrl+V**. You will find the cells pasted into your document as a Table, which you can add further enhancements.

If formulas are used to create values, you may get the error **#REF!** To paste correctly, choose **Edit**, **Paste Special**. Choose whether you want **Formulas** or **Values**.

Chapter 2 Computing Probabilities

Excel has a number of functions for computing probabilities. In this chapter we will show you how to work with the probability function of a binomial random variable, how to compute probabilities involving normal random variables.

2.1   Binomial Probabilities

A binomial experiment consists of a fixed number of trials, n. On each independent trial the outcome is success or failure, with the probability of success, p, being the same for each trial. The random variable X is the number of successes in n trials, so $x = 0, 1,...., n$. For this discrete random variable, the probability that $X = x$ is given by the probability function

$$P(X = x) = f(x) = \left(\frac{n!}{x!(n-x)!}\right) p^x (1-p)^{n-x}, \quad x = 0,1,...,n$$

We can compute these probabilities two ways: the hard way and the easy way.

2.1.1   Computing Binomial Probabilities Directly

Excel has a number of mathematical functions that make computation of formulas straightforward. Assume there are $n = 5$ trials, that the probability of success is $p = 0.3$, and that we want the probability of $x = 3$ successes. What we must compute is

$$P(X = 3) = f(3) = \left(\frac{5!}{3!(5-3)!}\right).3^3 (1-.3)^{5-3}$$

Eventually you will learn many shortcuts in Excel, but should you forget how to compute some mathematical or statistical quantity, there is a **Paste Function** (f_*) button on the Excel toolbar,

- Click on the **Paste Function** button, select **Math & Trig** in the first column, and scroll down the list of functions in the right-hand column. When you reach **Fact** you see that this function returns the factorial of a number.

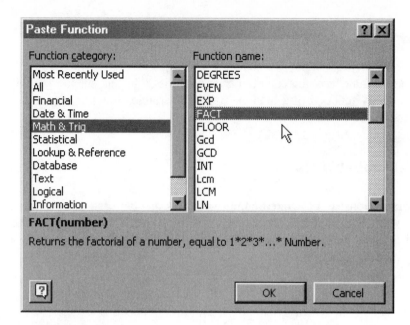

- Click **OK**. In the resulting dialog box, enter 5 and Excel determines that 5! = 120.

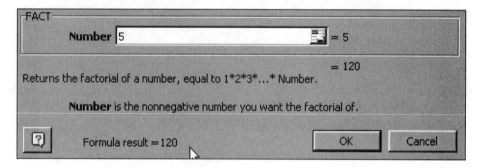

- Alternatively, click on **Help**. In the resulting dialog box, enter **factorial** and click **Search**

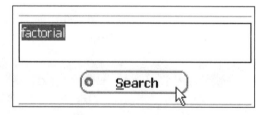

- Click on **FACT**.

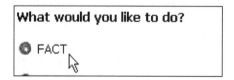

You are presented with an Excel function, **FACT(number)**, a definition and some examples.

The other mathematical operations we need to compute the binomial probability are multiplication (*), division (/) and power (^).

- In cell A1 type "f(3)", and in B1 type the formula

$$=(FACT(5)/(FACT(3)*FACT(2)))*(0.3^3)*(0.7^2)$$

It will look like

B1 ▼	=	=(FACT(5)/(FACT(3)*FACT(2)))*(0.3^3)*(0.7^2)
A		**B**
1 f(3)		=(FACT(5)/(FACT(3)*FACT(2)))*(0.3^3)*(0.7^2)

Note that we have used parentheses to group operations.
- Hit **<enter>**, and the result is 0.1323.

2.1.2 Computing Binomial Probabilities Using BINOMDIST

The Excel function **BINOMDIST** can be used to find either cumulative probability, $P(X \leq x)$ or the probability function, $P(X = x)$ for a Binomial random variable. Syntax for the function is

$$BINOMDIST(number\_s, trials, probability\_s, cumulative)$$

where   **number_s** is the number of successes in n trials
trials is the number of independent trials (n)
probability is p, the probability of success on any one trial
cumulative is a logical value. If set equal to 1 (true), the cumulative probability is returned; if set to 0 (false), the probability mass function is returned.

Access this function by clicking the **Paste Function** button. Select **Statistical** in the Function category and **BINOMDIST** in the Function name.

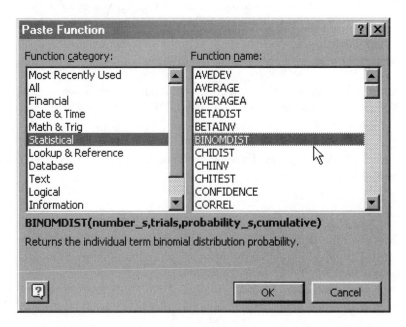

Using the values $n = 5$, $p = .3$, and $x = 3$ we obtain the probability 0.1323, as above.

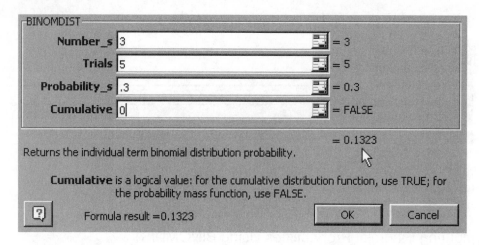

- Alternatively, we can type the function equation directly into a cell. For example, if $p = .2$ and $n = 10$, to find the probability that $X = 4$ and $X \le 4$, the worksheet would appears as follows:

| =BINOMDIST(4,10,0.2,0) | 0.08808 |
| =BINOMDIST(4,10,0.2,1) | 0.967207 |

The formulas in the first column produce the results reported in the second column.

2.2   The Normal Distribution

Excel provides several functions related to the Normal and Standard Normal Distributions.

1. The **STANDARDIZE** function computes the Z value for given values of X, μ, and σ. The format of this function is

$$STANDARDIZE(X, \mu, \sigma)$$

Referring to the example in Section 2.6 in which $\mu = 3$ and $\sigma = 3$, if we wanted to find the Z value corresponding to $X = 6$, we would enter =STANDARDIZE(6,3,3) in a cell, and the value computed would be 1.0.

2. The **NORMSDIST** function computes the area, or cumulative probability, less than a given Z value. Geometrically, the cumulative probability is

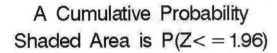

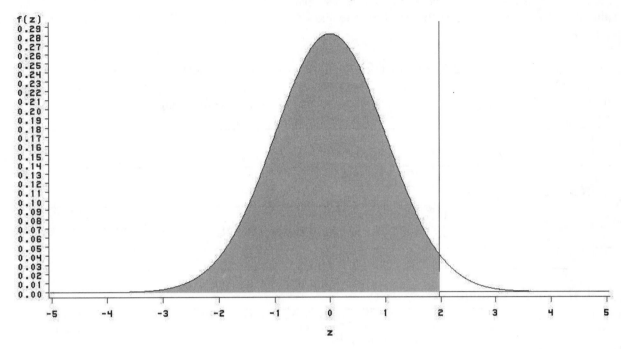

The format of this function is

NORMSDIST(Z)

If we wanted to find the area below a Z value of 1.0, we would enter =NORMSDIST(1.0) in a cell, and the value computed would be .8413.

3. The **NORMSINV** function computes the Z value corresponding to a given cumulative area under the normal curve. The format of this function is

NORMSINV(*prob*)

where ***prob*** is the area under the standard normal curve less than z. That is, $prob = P(Z < z)$.

If we wanted to find the z value corresponding to a cumulative area of .10, we would enter =NORMSINV(.10) in a cell and the value computed would be −1.2815.

4. The **NORMDIST** function computes the area or probability less than a given X value. The format of this function is

NORMDIST(X, μ, σ, TRUE)

TRUE is a logical value, which can be replaced by 1. If we wanted to find the area below an X value of 6, we would enter =NORMDIST(6,3,3,1) in a cell, and the value computed would be .8413.

5. The **NORMINV** function computes the x value corresponding to a cumulative area under the normal curve. The format of this function is

$$\text{NORMINV}(prob, \mu, \sigma)$$

where **prob** is the area under the normal curve less than x. That is, $prob = P(X < x)$. To compute the value of x such that .10 of the probability is to the left, enter =NORMINV(.10,3,3) in a cell, yielding −0.8446.

For the example in Section 2.6, a template can be built in Excel to compute probabilities and values of X corresponding to particular probabilities. The highlighted cells require user input. The formulas in the other cells do the computations. Set up a spreadsheet that looks like the following

	A	B
1	Normal Probabilities	
2	mean	
3	standard_dev	
4		
5	Left-tail Probability	
6	a	
7	P(X<=a)	=NORMDIST(B6,B2,B3,1)
8		
9	Right-tail Probability	
10	a	
11	P(X>=a)	=1-NORMDIST(B10,B2,B3,1)
12		
13	Interval Probability	
14	a	
15	b	
16	P(a<=X<=b)	=NORMDIST(B15,B2,B3,1)-NORMDIST(B14,B2,B3,1)
17		
18	Inverse cumulative	
19	Left-tail probability	
20	Quantile	=NORMINV(B19,B2,B3)

Using X~N(3,9), the above template would produce the following results:

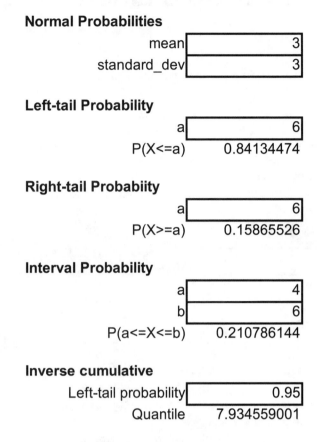

Normal Probabilities

mean	3
standard_dev	3

Left-tail Probability

a	6
P(X<=a)	0.84134474

Right-tail Probabiity

a	6
P(X>=a)	0.15865526

Interval Probability

a	4
b	6
P(a<=X<=b)	0.210786144

Inverse cumulative

Left-tail probability	0.95
Quantile	7.934559001

Note that the Quantile = 7.93 gives the top 5% "cut off" value.

Once again, if you forget these formulas, use the **Paste Function** (*f*∗) button on the Menu Bar.

Chapter 3 The Simple Linear Regression Model

In this Chapter you will learn to carry out regression analysis using Excel.

3.1   Import the Data

Following the steps outlined in Chapter 1, import the data file *table3-1.dat* into an Excel worksheet.

- Click on the open file button, 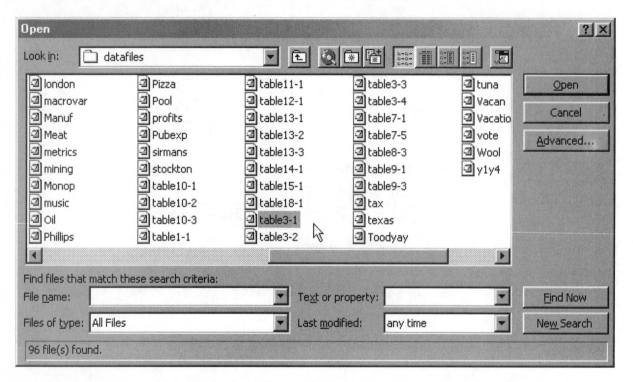.
- Assuming the data are in **c:\datafiles**, locate this subdirectory, and select the file.

- Proceed with the Wizard, recalling that data files in *UE/2* are **space delimited** ascii files, with the extension *.dat*.
- Save this as an Excel file in a folder with some logical name. We save the file as *ch3.xls* and place it in **c:\econometrics**.

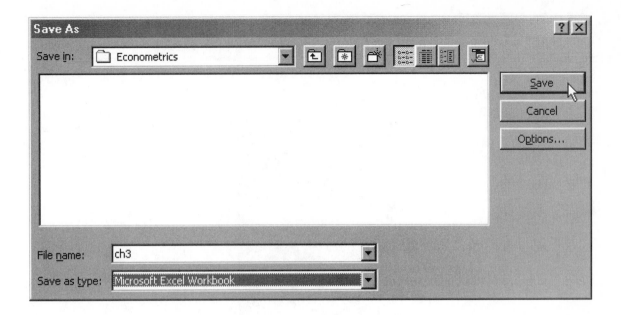

3.2   *Estimating the Food Expenditure Model*

3.2.1   Opening the Regression Dialog Box

Place cursor in an empty cell. Click on **Tools/Data Analysis**.

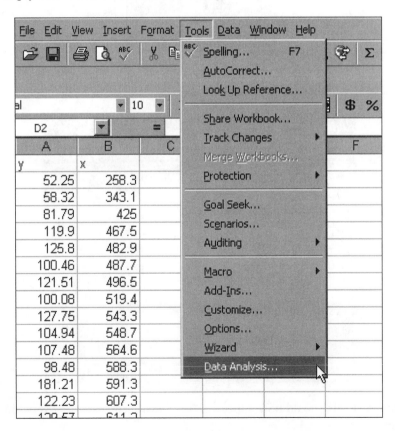

Note: The Data Analysis tool does not automatically load with a default installation of the program, but you DO NOT need the installation discs or CD to add it. If the Data Analysis tool doesn't appear on the menu, do the following

- Click on **Tools/Add-Ins**.

- Check the box next to the Analysis Toolpak add-in.

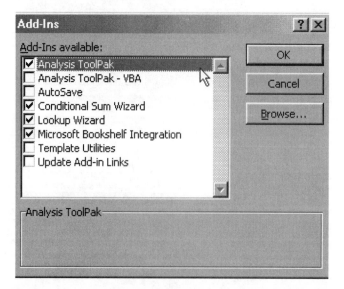

- Click **OK**. Data Analysis should now appear in the Tools menu, and you should not have to run the add-ins again for this option.

The Data Analysis dialog box will appear.

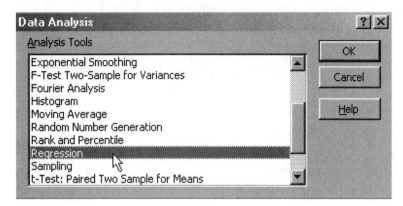

- Click on **Regression**, then **OK**. The Regression dialog box appears, with lots of user-defined inputs and options.

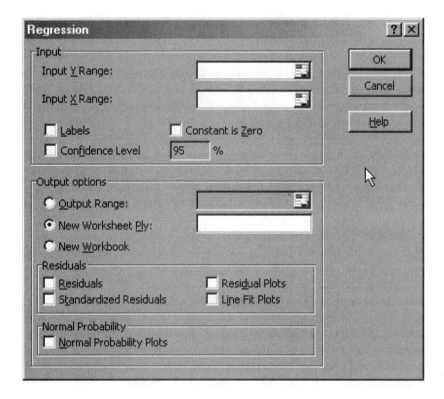

3.2.2 Specifying the Data Ranges

There are several ways you can input the Y and X ranges.

3.2.2(a)   *If the dialog box obscures the data*

- Click on the box with the red arrow in the Y Range box.
- The box will minimize. Highlight the data in the y column, including the label "y".
- Hit **Enter** or click on the box with the red arrow.

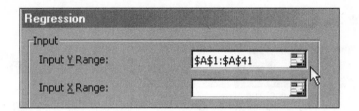

- Do the same procedure to input the X Range.

3.2.2(b)   *If the dialog box does not obscure the data*

If the data are not obscured by the dialog box, with the cursor in the appropriate box, simply highlight the data (including label). The data range will appear automatically.

3.2.3 Filling in the Options

- Check the Labels box, since you included labels with the data.
- Do not check the Constant is Zero box. This would suppress the intercept.

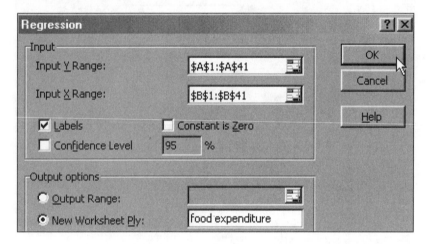

- The output can be sent to the current page, another page in the workbook, which can be named at this time (recommended), or to another, new workbook. If you choose a new page in the same workbook, the page will appear as a tab in the lower left corner of the work area.
- Do not worry about the other options at this time. Click **OK**. Excel does the least squares computations and puts a summary of the results on a new worksheet ply.
- Note the location of the cursor in the lower left. This workbook now has two "pages", or worksheets, named *table3-1* and *food expenditure*.

- Also, notice that the columns are not wide enough to show the cells completely. Highlight the data, or the entire sheet, and click on **Format/Column/Autofit Selection**.

Finally, formatted results will be

SUMMARY OUTPUT					
Regression Statistics					
Multiple R	0.563132517				
R Square	0.317118231				
Adjusted R Square	0.299147658				
Standard Error	37.80536423				
Observations	40				
ANOVA					
	df	*SS*	*MS*	*F*	*Significance F*
Regression	1	25221.22299	25221.22299	17.64652878	0.00015495
Residual	38	54311.33145	1429.245564		
Total	39	79532.55444			
	Coefficients	*Standard Error*	*t Stat*	*P-value*	*Lower 95%*
Intercept	40.76755647	22.13865442	1.841464964	0.073369453	-4.049807902
x	0.128288601	0.030539254	4.200777164	0.00015495	0.066465111

(Note that we have cut off some of the output from the right side.)

3.3   Graph of the Estimated Regression Function

In order to plot the regression function we must re-estimate the food expenditure equation and choose a new option.

- Choose the **Line Fit Plots** option in the regression dialog box.

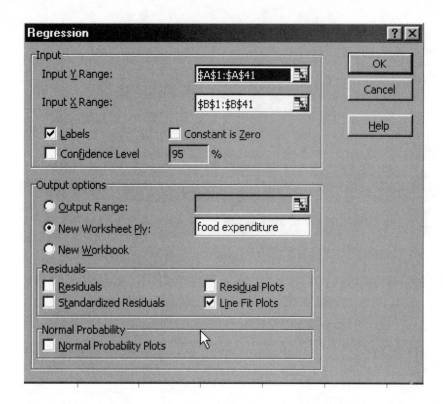

- Click **OK**. The graph will be produced, and placed on the same worksheet as the regression output. If you can't find it on the worksheet, click on the **File/Print Preview** or click on the Print Preview icon and look for it. It is there somewhere.

Some formatting is necessary.

- Right click on the legend and delete, if desired.

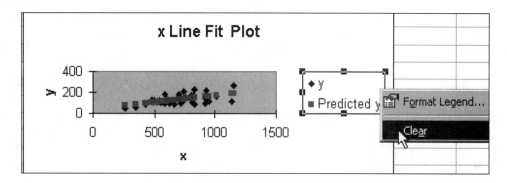

- Left click once on the title to highlight it. Left click once more to edit. Name appropriately. If you double click the box surrounding the title, a dialog box opens that allows you more formatting options.

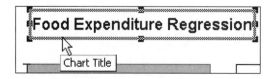

- Repeat for the Y and X axes.
- Notice that both the actual values of Y and the predicted values are plotted. To include the estimated regression function, place the cursor over one of the predicted Y points (the pink ones) until the caption "Series Predicted Y" appears.

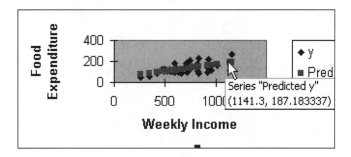

- **Right Click** and choose **Add Trendline**.

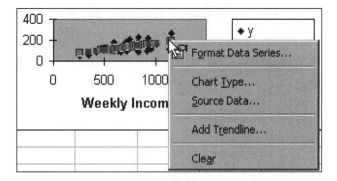

- Under the Type tab, choose **Linear**.

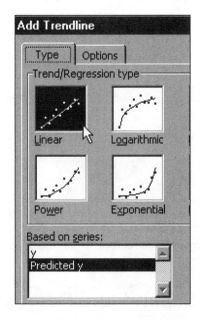

- Under the Options tab, check the box next to Display equation on chart. Click **OK**.

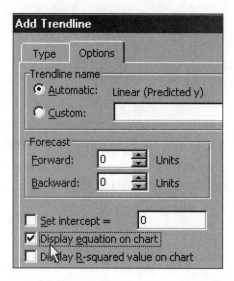

- If your figure is small, and begins to get cluttered at this point, increase its size by clicking inside the border.

- Place the mouse arrow over the black square in the corner, until a double arrow appears. Then drag the mouse, with the left button held down, to increase (or decrease) the figure size.

- The estimated equation may appear initially in the center of the graph.

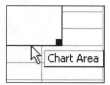

- Click on the equation border. Drag the mouse, with the left button held down, to place the equation under the title.

- To remove the pink predicted Y points, **Right Click** on any of the predicted points, choose **Format Data Series**.

- Under the **Patterns** tab, check **None** under Marker. Any further formatting can be done; resizing the plot area, setting font type and size for titles and labels, resizing the entire chart, etc.

Your figure should look something like the one below.

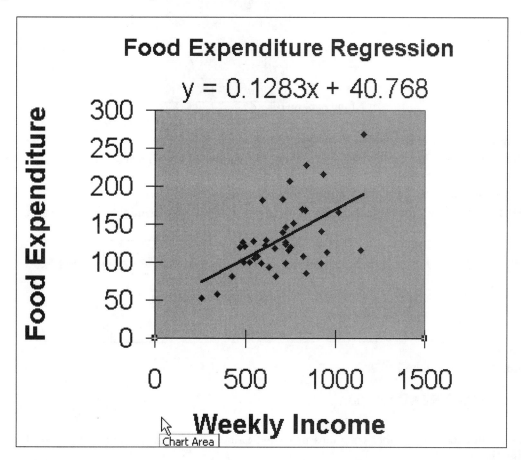

Each piece of the Microsoft Excel chart we've created can be edited, resized, colors selected, and so on. In Excel click on **Help** and scroll down to find **Working with Charts**. Click on this topic and you will find extensive help.

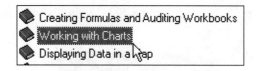

3.4   Predicting from the Estimated Regression Function

Obtaining predicted values from an estimated regression function is quite straightforward. Simply let Excel do the number crunching.

3.4.1 Doing the Computations

- Insert a new worksheet to the workbook by right clicking on a page tab near the lower left corner. Choose **Insert, Worksheet, OK**.

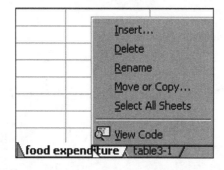

- Rename the worksheet **Predictions** by right clicking on the tab.
- Create a template for prediction by copying the estimated coefficients from the regression and labeling them appropriately.
- Enter the income value for which you want to predict food expenditures.
- Create the formula for the predicted value of y, $\hat{y} = b_1 + b_2 Income$, using the cell references.

Predicted Food Expenditure	
b1	40.7675564655779
b2	0.128288601052181
income	=750
Yhat	=B3+(B4*B5)

The results in cell B6 will be 136.984.

3.4.2 Using the **TREND** function

Excel has a built in function that computes predicted values from simple regressions. The form of the **Trend function** is

TREND(*range of Y variable, range of X variable, value of x₀*)

The value x_0 is the value at which the prediction is desired. To use this function, return to the worksheet page containing the data. Type in the following command,

y	x		
52.25	258.3	yhat	=TREND(A2:A41,B2:B41,750)
58.32	343.1		

The result is

C	D
yhat	136.9840073

Chapter 4 Properties of the Least Squares Estimators

In this Chapter we discuss how to obtain estimates of the variances and the standard errors of the least squares estimators.

4.1   The Least Squares Residuals

Open the workbook *ch3.xls* that we created in Chapter 3. If you did not save it, follow the steps in Chapter 3.1 to import the data from *table3-1.dat*.

Following the steps in Chapter 3.2, estimate the food expenditure model, choosing the option to compute the least squares residuals. The regression dialog box will look like this.

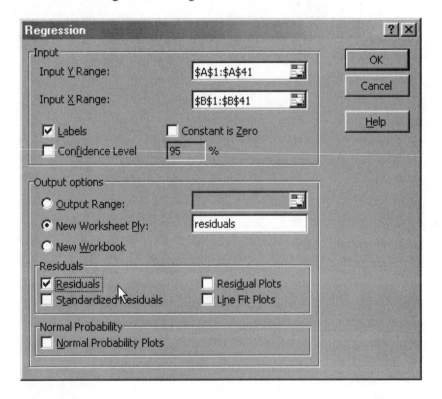

Note we have checked the box labeled **Residuals**, and we have also specified a new worksheet ply as the destination for the output.

In addition to the regression output, we now have the **RESIDUAL OUTPUT**, which gives for each observation the fitted value of y, $\hat{y} = b_1 + b_2 x$, and the least squares residual, $\hat{e}_t = y_t - \hat{y}_t$. Some of the output is shown on the next page.

28

22	RESIDUAL OUTPUT		
23			
24	Observation	Predicted y	Residuals
25	1	73.90450212	-21.65450212
26	2	84.78337549	-26.46337549
27	3	95.29021191	-13.50021191
28	4	100.7424775	19.15752254
29	5	102.7181219	23.08187809
30	6	103.3339072	-2.873907199
31	7	104.4628469	17.04715311
32	8	107.4006559	-7.320655852
33	9	110.4667534	17.28324658
34	10	111.1595119	-6.219511863

4.2   *Estimating the Error Variance,* $\hat{\sigma}^2$

In the simple linear model the variance of the error term is $\text{var}(e_t) = \sigma^2$. To estimate this parameter we divide the sum of squared least squares residuals $\sum \hat{e}_t^2$ by the degrees of freedom, T–2, so that

$$\hat{\sigma}^2 = \frac{\sum \hat{e}_t^2}{T-2}$$

To compute the sum of squared residuals proceed as follows:
- In cell D25, square the value in cell C25 by typing, **=C25^2** then **<enter>**.

A	B	C	D
RESIDUAL OUTPUT			
Observation	Predicted y	Residuals	
	1	73.90450212	-21.65450212	=C25^2

- Click on the **Copy** icon. Note that the cell is "activated." Put the cursor on the lower right hand corner of the cell. You will see a + appear.

Residuals	
-21.65450212	468.917462
-26.46337549	

- While holding the left button down, drag the mouse down to cell D64. This copies the **formula** in cell D25 to all the other cells, substituting in the correct address for the quantity being squared.

Predicted y	Residuals	
73.9045021173561	-21.6545021173561	=C25^2
84.7833754865811	-26.4633754865811	=C26^2
95.2902119127547	-13.5002119127547	=C27^2
100.742477457472	19.1575225425276	=C28^2
102.718121913676	23.0818780863241	=C29^2
103.333907198726	-2.87390719872641	=C30^2

- In cell D65, sum the squared residuals. To do this click on the paste function (f_x), and choose **Sum**. Fill in the appropriate range and click **OK**.

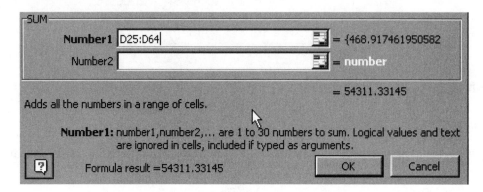

- Or, simply type **=SUM(D25:D64)** in the cell. You may consider "marking" this cell for future reference, such as placing a border around the cell. The result is 54311.33145, which represents $\sum \hat{e}_t^2$.

We can then calculate

$$\hat{\sigma}^2 = \frac{\sum \hat{e}_t^2}{T-2} = \frac{54311.33145}{38} = 1429.245564$$

This quantity is so important it is reported automatically in the ANOVA (Analysis of Variance) table when a regression is estimated.

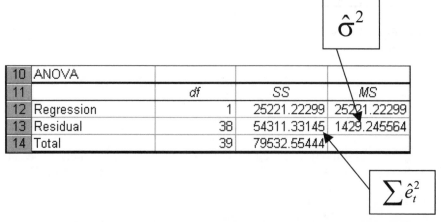

10	ANOVA			
11		df	SS	MS
12	Regression	1	25221.22299	25221.22299
13	Residual	38	54311.33145	1429.245564
14	Total	39	79532.55444	

The contents of this table are more fully explained in Chapter 6. The column labeled "*SS*" contains various "sums of squares", the *df* column contains degrees of freedom, and the "*MS*" column, standing for "mean squares," is the ratio *SS/df*. If we use the numbers in the "Residual" row, we see that the computed value is $\hat{\sigma}^2$.

Furthermore, under *Regression Statistics*, the **Standard Error** is the estimated standard error of the model. As you can verify, squaring this value gives 1429.245564, is the estimated variance of the error term.

$$\hat{\sigma} = \sqrt{\frac{\sum \hat{e}_t^2}{T-2}} = 37.80536423$$

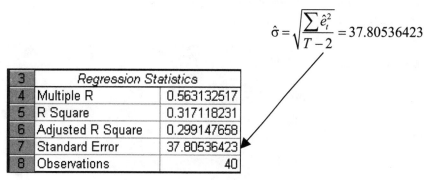

3	Regression Statistics	
4	Multiple R	0.563132517
5	R Square	0.317118231
6	Adjusted R Square	0.299147658
7	Standard Error	37.80536423
8	Observations	40

4.3   The Variances and Covariances of the Least Squares Estimators

The estimated variances and covariances of the least squares estimators are not directly reported in Excel. However, in the simple model they are easily obtained. The estimated variance of b_2 is

$$\hat{var}(b_2) = \frac{\hat{\sigma}^2}{\sum\limits_{t=1}^{T}(x_t - \overline{x})^2}$$

The standard error of the estimated coefficient is

$$se(b_2) = \sqrt{\hat{var}(b_2)} = \sqrt{\frac{\hat{\sigma}^2}{\sum\limits_{t=1}^{T}(x_t - \overline{x})^2}}$$

In the Excel output we are given the values of the standard errors for the least squares estimates.

16		Coefficients	Standard Error
17	Intercept	40.76755647	22.13865442
18	x	0.128288601	0.030539254

The standard errors are reported in the column next to the coefficient estimates. The estimated variances can be obtained by squaring the standard errors.

The estimated covariances of the least squares estimators are not reported by Excel. For the simple regression model, with only one explanatory variable, calculating the covariance is not difficult. The formula for the covariance (or the variances) can be "translated" into an Excel formula.

$$\hat{\text{cov}}(b_1, b_2) = \hat{\sigma}^2 \left[\frac{-\bar{x}}{\sum (x_t - \bar{x})^2} \right]$$

- From the regression worksheet, copy the standard error of the model to the worksheet containing the original data. Square the value, and label the cell.
- To compute the sample mean of the *x* values we can using an Excel function. Click on the paste function icon (*f_x*). Find the statistical function **AVERAGE**.

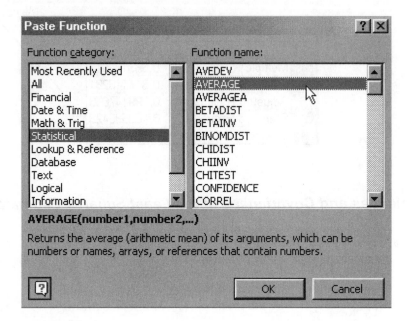

Include the range and click **OK**.

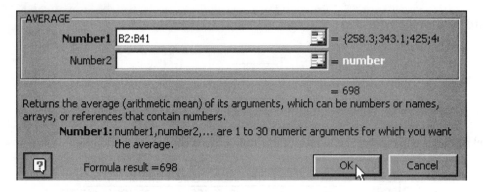

Or you can enter the formula directly.

=AVERAGE(B2:B41)		
C	D	E
	sigmahat2	xbar
	1429.245564	698

- In column E, create a column, *x – xbar*, by typing in the first empty cell of the column **=B2-$D$2**, where B2 contains the first value of *x*, and D2 contains *xbar*. The dollar sign in the formula "anchors" the cell reference; when the formula is copied, the value in D2 will copy across the cells. Copy the formula down the column to include all observations of *x*.

- Label the next column *SSQ*. Click on the paste function and select the math function **SUMSQ**

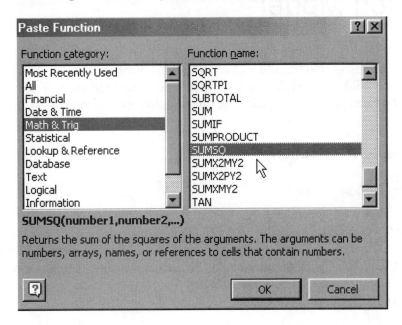

Enter the range of the data corresponding to the *x-xbar* column. We obtain the result that

$$\sum_{t=1}^{T}(x_t - \overline{x})^2 = 1532463.02$$

Now compute the estimated variance of b_2 and the covariance between b_1 and b_2. For example,

- In a new cell labeled *cov(b1,b2)*, "translate" the formula for the covariance into Excel by typing **=C2*(-D2/F2)**, and the result is -.6510. A portion of the worksheet to obtain this result is provided below, showing both the formulas used, and the results.

F	G	H	I
ssq	varb2	seb2	cov(b1,b2)
=SUMSQ(E2:E41)	=C2/F2	=SQRT(G2)	=-C2*D2/F2

ssq	varb2	seb2	cov(b1,b2)
1532463	0.000932646	0.030539	-0.65099

Note: The calculation of the estimated covariance of the least squares estimators is done here using only one explanatory variable. A more complex model would require calculations beyond the scope of this book.

Chapter 5 Inference in the Simple Regression Model

Inference in the linear regression model includes interval estimation of parameters, tests of hypotheses about parameters, and prediction intervals. Each of these depends upon Student's *t*-distribution. In this chapter we present the Excel functions related to the *t*-distribution and use them as a basis for carrying out other inference tasks.

5.1   The Student-t Distribution

5.1.1   Computing Critical Values

Excel makes it easy to compute critical values from the *t*-distribution. We want values t_c, such that $\alpha/2$ of the probability is in either tail, as shown in Figure 5.3 in *UE/2*. As an example, let us find the critical values that mark off $\alpha/2 = .025$ of the probability in each tail of a *t*-distribution with 20 degrees of freedom. Checking Table 2 at the front of the book, we find that the value is $t_c = 2.086$ on the positive side and, using the symmetry of the *t-distribution*, -2.086 on the negative side.

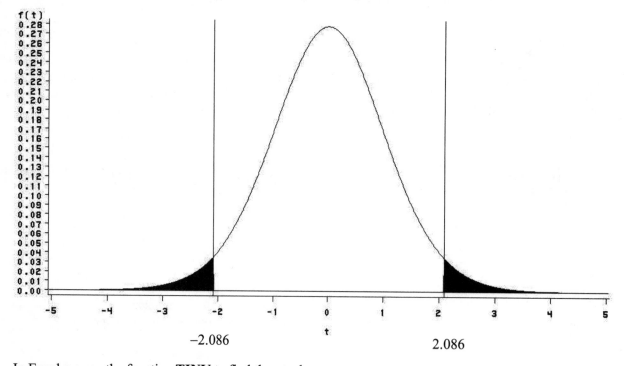

Student t—Distribution with 20 degrees of freedom
Critical Values for alpha = .05

-2.086 2.086

In Excel we use the function **TINV** to find these values.

34

- Open the workbook containing the food expenditure regression (*ch3.xls*), or create the workbook as in Chapter 3.
- Click on **Insert/Worksheet**. Move the cursor over the tab with the default name, right click, and rename the sheet **t-values**.
- Select a cell. Click on the **Paste Function** button (*f**). Choose the function **TINV** from the Statistical Function category, and click **OK**.

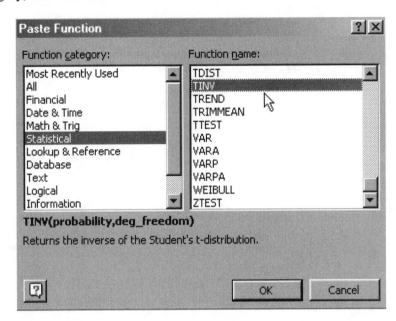

- Fill in the resulting dialog box as shown below.

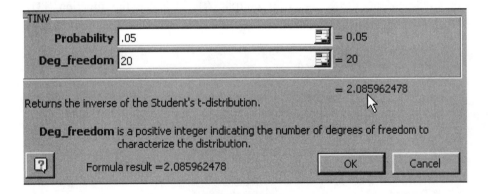

The **Probability** value it asks for is the value α in **two-tails** of the *t*-distribution. Enter the degrees of freedom, 20, and click **OK**. The resulting value **2.085962** is rounded off less than the values given in Table 2 in *UE/2*.

5.1.2 Computing Tail Probabilities

The other calculation that is important is the computation of tail probabilities. For example, in a *t*-distribution with 20 degrees of freedom, how much probability is to the **right** of the value $t = 1.90$? The desired probability is the shaded area in the Figure below.

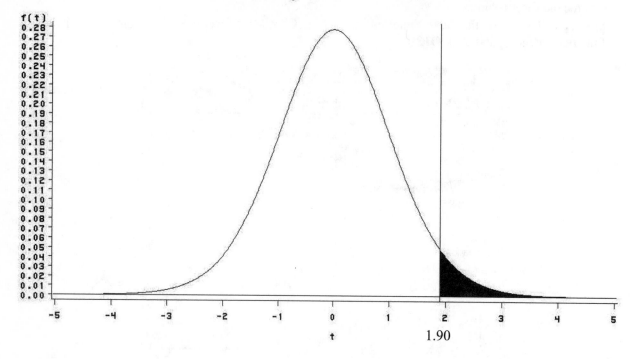

To compute this probability we use the Excel function **TDIST**.

- Select a cell. Click on the **Paste Function** button (*f*$_*$).   Choose the function **TDIST** from the Statistical Function category, and click **OK**.

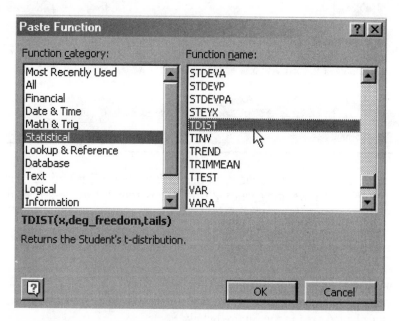

- Fill in the resulting dialog box as shown below.

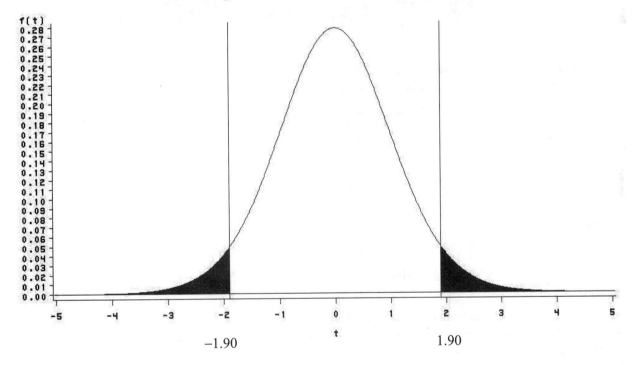

If you specify **Tails** to be 1, then the function returns the probability to the **right** of the given value, 0.035974. If you specify **Tails** to be 2, then the returned value is 0.071948, which is the area in the following figure.

Student t−Distribution with 20 degrees of freedom
Probability that t < −1.90 or t > 1.90

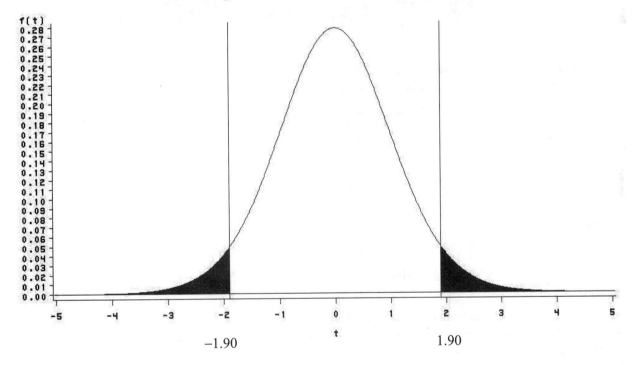

5.2   *Interval Estimation*

5.2.1 Automatic Interval Estimates

The Regression function in Excel can quickly and easily calculate interval estimates for the least squares parameters.

- Open the workbook containing the food expenditures regression (*ch3.xls*), or create the workbook as in Chapter 3.

- By default, Excel provides a 95% confidence interval for the LS estimates.

	Coefficients	Standard Error	t Stat	P-value	Lower 95%	Upper 95%
17 Intercept	40.76755647	22.13865442	1.841464964	0.073369453	-4.049807902	85.58492083
18 x	0.128288601	0.030539254	4.200777164	0.00015495	0.066465111	0.190112091

- To have Excel calculate a 98% confidence interval, run a regression and, in the dialog box, check the **Confidence Level** box. Type in the desired level, 98.

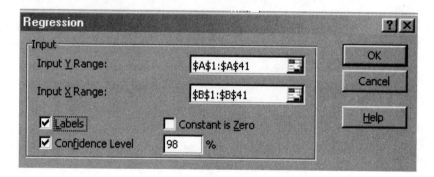

The results show the lower and upper values for the 95% confidence interval (always by default), and the lower and upper values for the 98% confidence interval for both b_1 and b_2.

Lower 98.0%	Upper 98.0%
-12.99769629	94.53280923
0.054121911	0.202455291

While this is the quickest and easiest way to obtain interval estimates, a general template can be created for calculating interval estimates. This is especially useful when you are interested in the margin of error, or **half-width**, $t_c \text{se}(b_k)$.

5.2.2 Constructing Interval Estimates

- Insert a new worksheet and call it **Interval_Template**.
- Create the following template. Cells with bold border require user input, some obtained from the regression results.

	A	B
1	Interval Estimation Using the t-distribution	
2		
3	**Data Input**	
4	Sample Size	
5	Conf_Level	
6	Estimate Value	
7	StdError	
8	**Computed Values**	
9	df	=B4-2
10	t	=TINV(1-B5,B4-2)
11	half_width	=B10*B7
12	**Confidence Interval**	
13	Lower Limit	=B6-B11
14	Upper Limit	=B6+B11

Calculation of a 98% interval estimate for β_2 would appear as

	A	B
1	Interval Estimation Using the t-distribution	
2		
3	**Data Input**	
4	Sample Size	40
5	Conf_Level	0.98
6	Estimate Value	0.128289
7	StdError	0.030539
8	**Computed Values**	
9	df	38
10	t	2.428569
11	half_width	0.074167
12	**Confidence Interval**	
13	Lower Limit	0.054122
14	Upper Limit	0.202455

Note: The estimate value and the StdError values can be typed in, or can be copied from the regression results on the food expenditure worksheet. To copy these values

- Select the cell containing the value in the **food expenditure** worksheet.
- Click on the copy icon, or Strike **Ctrl+C**.
- Click on the tab returning you to the **Interval_Template** worksheet.
- Select the cell where the value is to go.
- Click **Edit/Paste Special** and select **Values**.
- Click **OK**.

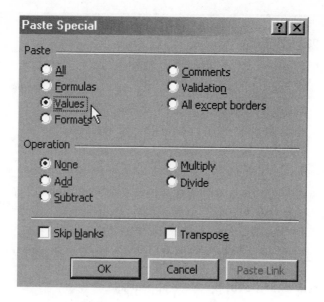

5.3   General Hypothesis Testing

One- or two-tailed general tests can be calculated by methods similar to the confidence interval construction in Chapter 5.2. The required ingredients are results from the least squares estimation and the ability to use the Excel functions **TINV** and **TDIST**.

5.3.1 Construction of Two-Tailed Test Results

If we wish to test the null hypothesis $H_0 : \beta_2 = c$ against the alternative that $H_1 : \beta_2 \neq c$, then we use a two-tailed test. We must compute the value of the test statistic, and the critical values that define the rejection region, as shown in Figure 5.4 of *UE/2*. Further, we wish to compute the *p*-value of the test.

Let us use the example illustrated in Figure 5.5 of *UE/2*, based on a test of the hypothesis $H_0 : \beta_2 = .10$ against $H_1 : \beta_2 \neq 10$.

- Insert a new worksheet called **t-test**.
Compute the value of the test statistic

$$t = \frac{b_2 - .10}{se(b_2)} = 0.926303$$

- Copy and paste (use **Edit/Paste Special/Values**) the values of the estimate and its standard error from the regression output

	A	B
1	2 tailed t-test	
2	b2	0.128288601052181
3	seb2	0.0305392540557929
4	t	=(B2-0.1)/B3

The critical value for the two-tailed test is computed using the **TINV** function discussed in Chapter 5.1.1 of this handbook. For $\alpha = .05$ and 38 degrees of freedom, enter the expression

- =TINV(0.05,38)

This returns the positive critical value 2.024394.

For the *p*-value, we use the **TDIST** function discussed in Chapter 5.1.2. We wish to compute the amount of probability in the 2-tails of a *t*-distribution with 38 degrees of freedom.

- Using the **Paste Function** button, select **TDIST**, and enter the information as shown.

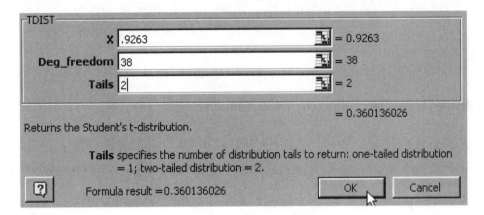

The resulting *p*-value is 0.360136.

5.3.2 Construction of One-Tailed (>) Test Results

If we wish to test the null hypothesis $H_0 : \beta_2 = c$ against the alternative that $H_1 : \beta_2 > c$, then we use a one-tailed test. We must compute the value of the test statistic, and the critical values that define the rejection region, as shown in Figure 5.8 of *UE/2*. Further, we wish to compute the *p*-value of the test.

Let us test the hypothesis $H_0 : \beta_2 = .10$ against $H_1 : \beta_2 > 10$. The value of the *t*-statistic for this null and alternative hypothesis is the same as for a two-tailed test.

The critical value for this one-tailed test is computed using the **TINV** function discussed in Chapter 5.1.1 of this handbook. For $\alpha = .05$ and 38 degrees of freedom, enter the expression

- =TINV(0.10,38)

This returns the right tail critical value 1.685953. Some explanation is needed here. The Excel function **TINV(*probability, degrees of freedom*)** returns the value such that the area in the *two-tails* of the *t(df)* distribution equals the given *probability* value. Thus if we want a critical value such that $\alpha = .05$ is in the right tail, we must provide the TINV function with *probability* = .10.

For the *p*-value, we use the **TDIST** function discussed in Chapter 5.1.2. We wish to compute the amount of probability in the right-tail of a *t*-distribution with 38 degrees of freedom.

- Using the **Paste Function** button, select **TDIST**, and enter the information as shown.

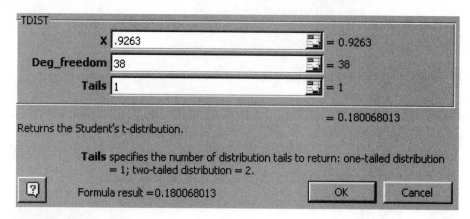

The resulting p-value is 0.180068.

5.3.3 Construction of One-Tailed (<) Test Results

Let us test the hypothesis $H_0 : \beta_2 = .10$ against $H_1 : \beta_2 < 10$. The value of the t-statistic for this null and alternative hypothesis is the same as for a two-tailed test. The critical value for this one-tailed test is depicted in the next figure.

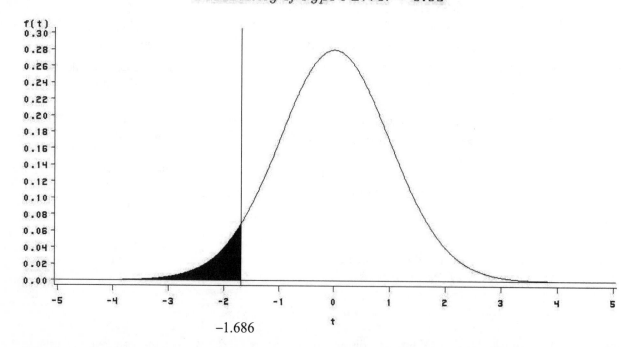

We can compute the critical value using the **TINV** function, but it requires us to understand the location of the rejection region.

For α = .05 and 38 degrees of freedom, enter the expression (the logic of which is explained in Chapter 5.2.2).

- =TINV(0.10,38)

This returns the **right** tail critical value 1.685953. Since we need the left-tail critical value we use the symmetry of the *t*-distribution and conclude that the critical value is −1.685953.

For the *p*-value, we use the **TDIST** function but we must remember that this function returns the area in the **right**-tail of a *t*-distribution with 38 degrees of freedom. For a hypothesis test with an alternative that is "less than," we compute the *p*-value in the **left** tail of the *t*-distribution.

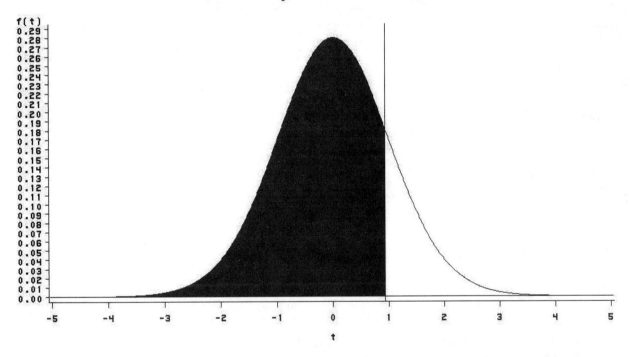

- Using the **Paste Function** button, select **TDIST**, and enter the information as shown.

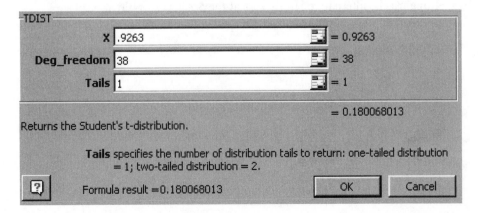

The resulting value is 0.180068. The *p*-value is 1–0.180068=0.819932.

5.3.4 A Template for Test Results

All the above work can be simplified by using a template that can be used over and over.

- In a new worksheet, create the following template. Shaded cells require user input, some obtained from the regression results (use **Copy/Edit/Paste Special/Values**).

	A	B
1	Hypothesis Testing Using the t-Distribution	
2	**Data Input**	
3	Sample size	
4	Estimate	
5	StdError	
6	Ho	
7	Alpha	
8	**Computed Values**	
9	df	=B3-2
10	t	=(B4-B6)/B5
11	**Left-Tail Test**	
12	Left Critical Value	=-TINV(2*B7,B9)
13	Decision	=IF(B10<=B12,"Reject Ho","Do Not Reject Ho")
14	p-value	=IF(B10<0,TDIST(ABS(B10),B9,1),1-TDIST(ABS(B10),B9,1))
15	**Right-Tail Test**	
16	Right Critical Value	=TINV(2*B7,B9)
17	Decision	=IF(B10>=B16,"Reject Ho","Do Not Reject Ho")
18	p-value	=IF(B10>0,TDIST(B10,B9,1),1-TDIST(ABS(B10),B9,1))
19	**Two-Tail Test**	
20	Absolute Critical Value	=TINV(B7,B9)
21	Decision	=IF(OR(B10<=-B20,B10>=B20),"Reject Ho","Do Not Reject Ho")
22	p-value	=TDIST(ABS(B10),B9,2)

This template can now be used to test any type of null and alternative hypotheses, one-tailed or two-tailed. Simply disregard any output not desired.

The test H_0: $\beta_2 = .1$ against the alternative H_1: $\beta_2 \neq .1$ at the 5% level would appear as

	A	B
1	Hypothesis Testing Using the t-Distribution	
2	**Data Input**	
3	Sample size	40
4	Estimate	0.128288601
5	StdError	0.030539254
6	Ho	0.1
7	Alpha	0.05
8	**Computed Values**	
9	df	38
10	t	0.926302948
11	**Left-Tail Test**	
12	Left Critical Value	-1.685953066
13	Decision	Do Not Reject Ho
14	p-value	0.819932743
15	**Right-Tail Test**	
16	Right Critical Value	1.685953066
17	Decision	Do Not Reject Ho
18	p-value	0.180067257
19	**Two-Tail Test**	
20	Absolute Critical Value	2.024394234
21	Decision	Do Not Reject Ho
22	p-value	0.360134514

Decision for
$H_0: \beta_2 = .1$ vs.
$H_1: \beta_2 \neq .1$

5.3.5 Tests of Significance

While the template created in the last section can be used for a test of significance, Excel regression output provides the t-stats and p-values necessary for testing $H_0: \beta_k = 0$ against the alternative $H_1: \beta_k \neq 0$. This portion of the regression output is shown below.

	Coefficients	Standard Error	t Stat	P-value
Intercept	40.7675565	22.13865442	1.84146496	0.0733695
X=Weekly Income	0.1282886	0.030539254	4.20077716	0.000155

The reported t-stats for both b_1 and b_2 are equal to the coefficient divided by the corresponding standard error. The reported *p*-value is based on a two-tailed test. Based on these results, β_2 is significant at, essentially, any level, while β_1 is significant at the 10% level only.

5.4   *Prediction*

Predicting food expenditures for any given level of income was discussed in Chapter 3. For an income level of $750, we found $\hat{y}_0 = 40.7676 + .1283(750) = 136.98$

To find the interval estimate for $\hat{y}_0$, we must first calculate the standard error of the forecast, f.

$$se(f) = \sqrt{\widehat{var}(f)} = \sqrt{\hat{\sigma}^2 \left(1 + \frac{1}{T} + \frac{(x_0 - \bar{x})^2}{\sum(x_t - \bar{x})^2} \right)}.$$

While not directly provided by regression results in Excel, this calculation can be "manually".

- Return to the worksheet containing the original data. The data are in Columns A-B
- In the cell F2, calculate $\bar{x}$ as =AVERAGE(B2:B41). .
- Create column C of $(x_t - \bar{x})^2$ by typing in C2 =(B2-$F$2)^2, where B2 contains the first observation of income, and F2 contains the mean of income. Copy the formula down the column.
- Fill in the remaining cells in columns E-F as shown below

E	F
yhat	=TREND(A2:A41,B2:B41,750)
xbar	=AVERAGE(B2:B41)
x0	750
(x0-xbar)^2	=(F3-F2)^2
ssq_x	=SUMSQ(C2:C41)
sigmahat2	1429.24556442015
Sample Size	40
var(f)	=F6*(1+(1/F7)+(F4/F5))
se(f)	=SQRT(F8)

- The result is

yhat	136.9840073
xbar	698
x0	750
(x0-xbar)^2	2704
ssq_x	1532463.02
sigmahat2	1429.245564
Sample Size	40
var(f)	1467.498578
se(f)	38.30794406

- The template created for confidence intervals can now be used, where the Estimate value is now $\hat{y}_0$ = 136.9840073 and StdError is $se(f)$ = 38.30794406.

	A	B
1	Interval Estimation Using the t-distribution	
2		
3	**Data Input**	
4	Sample Size	40
5	Conf_Level	0.95
6	Estimate Value	136.9840073
7	StdError	38.30794406
8	**Computed Values**	
9	df	38
10	t	2.024394234
11	half_width	77.5503811
12	**Confidence Interval**	
13	Lower Limit	59.43362616
14	Upper Limit	214.5343884

Chapter 6 The Simple Linear Regression Model: Reporting the Results and Choosing the Functional Form

To complete the analysis of the simple linear regression model, we need to consider some of the statistics provided by the regression results, such as the ANOVA (which stands for the statistics term Analysis of Variance) table and the Summary Output. In addition, we should carefully consider the scale of our variables, the functional form of the relationship between the dependent and independent variable, and the assumption of normality of the error term. In this chapter, we will examine Excel's ANOVA results, show how to scale and transform the data when desirable, help decide on a particular functional form for the model, and use Excel to test for normality.

6.1 ANOVA and Coefficient of Determination

6.1.1 Regression ANOVA Results

In general, the following information is provided by the ANOVA table in simple regression output:

ANOVA					
Source of Variation	DF	Sum of Squares	Mean Square	F-stat	p-value
Explained	1	SSR	MSR=SSR/1	MSR/MSE	$P(F_{df1,df2} > F)$
Unexplained	T-2	SSE	MSE=SSE/(T-2)		
Total	T-1	SST			

For now, ignore the two columns on the right side.

- Open the workbook containing the food expenditure regression (ch3.xls), or create the workbook as in Chapter 3. By default, when a regression is performed, various summary values area reported in a so-called ANOVA table.

ANOVA

	df	SS	MS	F	Significance F
Regression	1	25221.223	25221.223	17.6465	0.00015495
Residual	38	54311.331	1429.2456		
Total	39	79532.554			

Using Excel terminology, note that

> SSR=Sum Square Regression and MSR=Mean Square Regression
> SSE=Sum Square Residual and MSE=Mean Square Residual

Excel calls the least squares residuals just "residuals".

R^2, the coefficient of determination can be calculated from this table. $R^2 = $ SSR/SST.

- In an empty cell, type the formula **=C12/C14**, where C12 refers to the cell where SSR is located and C14 is where SST is located. The result is 0.317118231.

Note: The estimated variance of the error term, $\hat{\sigma}^2 = $ SSE/(T-2) = MSE = 1429.2456 is reported in the ANOVA table.

6.1.2 Regression Summary Output

The first results presented in Excel regression are the Summary Output.

SUMMARY OUTPUT

Regression Statistics	
Multiple R	0.563132517
R Square	0.317118231
Adjusted R Square	0.299147658
Standard Error	37.80536423
Observations	40

There are several items of interest at this point.
1. R Square (R^2) is automatically calculated here. Note that the entry equals the result we found above.
2. Multiple R is the square root of R^2
3. Standard Error represents the estimated standard error (or "the standard error of the regression, or of the model"). This is equal to $\hat{\sigma} = \sqrt{\hat{\sigma}^2}$ which is $\sqrt{\text{MSE}}$, found in the ANOVA table. Verify this result.

- In the empty cell next the to standard error, type **=B7^2**. Cell B7 contains the standard error. The result is 1429.245564.
- Alternatively, in an empty cell, type **=SQRT(D13)**. Cell D13 contains the MSE from the ANOVA table. The result is 37.80536423.

4. Observations is the total sample size, T.

6.2 Covariance and Correlation Analysis

The covariance and correlation can tell us about the linear relationship between two variables, a primary concern of linear regression. Specifically, the covariance tells us the direction of the linear relationship, while the correlation is a measure of the strength (and direction) of the linear relationship. One should always investigate these measures when considering a linear regression.

6.2.1 The Covariance Function

- Return to the worksheet containing the original data.

- Click on **Tools/Data Analysis/Covariance**.

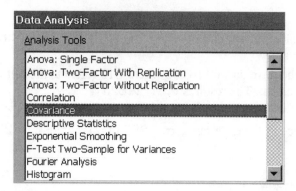

- Click **OK**. The covariance dialog appears. Fill in the appropriate input. Be sure to check the **Labels in First Row** box if labels are included (recommended). Place the output on a new worksheet named **cov**.

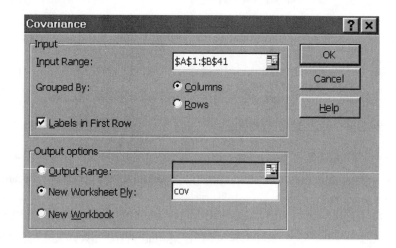

- Click **OK**.
- The covariance matrix will appear on the new worksheet, but needs to be formatted.   Choose **Format/Column/Auto Fit Selection**.

	A	B	C
1		Y=Food Expenditure	X=Weekly Income
2	Y=Food Expenditure	2039.296268	
3	X=Weekly Income	5040.962487	39293.92359
4			

Including the variable labels is recommended because they appear in the output. If they were not included, the labels would simply be Column1 and Column2, which can be confusing when you don't remember which variable is in which column.

The diagonal elements of the covariance matrix are the estimated sample variances, as given in equation 6.1.10b in *UE/2*. The covariance, from equation 6.1.10a, between food expenditures and weekly income is positive, suggesting a positive linear relationship. The value of the covariance, 5040.962, does not, however, tell you the strength of that linear relationship.

6.2.2 The Correlation Function

The sample correlation coefficient, r, measures the direction and strength of the linear relationship between two variables and is between -1 and 1. Its formula is in equation 6.1.11 in *UE/2*. To obtain the sample correlation coefficient, follow the instructions above for the correlation, except choose correlation from the **Tool/Data Analysis** menu.

- Click on **Tools/Data Analysis/Correlation**.

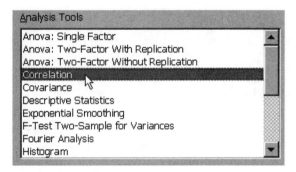

- Fill in the dialog box and click **OK**.

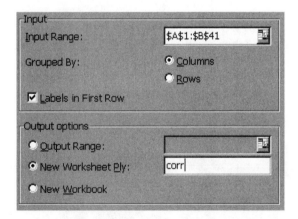

The results will appear in the new worksheet, **corr**. Again, you will need to format by choosing **Format/Column/AutoFit Selection**.

	A	B	C
1		Y=Food Expenditure	X=Weekly Income
2	Y=Food Expenditure	1	
3	X=Weekly Income	0.563132517	1

Note: Values on the diagonal of the correlation matrix will always equal 1.

The estimated correlation between food expenditures and weekly income, r, is .563, which is the value given as Multiple R in the regression output summary. R^2, the coefficient of determination is equal to r^2, the coefficient of correlation. This is only true in the simple regression model.

- In an empty cell on the worksheet **corr**, type **=B3^2**. The result is 0.317118231, which is the value reported for R Square in the Summary Output from the regression results.

A relationship that is always true, in simple linear regression and in the multiple regression models we consider later, is that R^2 is the square of the simple correlation between the values of y and their predicted values, $\hat{y}$. This point is made in Chapter 6.1.2 of *UE/2*.

6.3 Scaling the Data

If you want to change the units of measure of the variables, this is easily done on the worksheet containing the data.

6.3.1 Changing the Scale of x

- If necessary, create an empty column to the right of the independent variable by clicking on the column letter to the right of Weekly Income. Choose **Insert/Columns**.

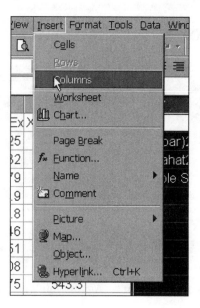

- Label this new column **x***.
- In the first empty cell of this column, type **=B2/100**.
- Copy the formula down the column.
- Run a regression, using the new independent variable, **x***. Results are

	Coefficients	Standard Error	t Stat	P-value	Lower 95%	Upper 95%
Intercept	40.76755647	22.13865442	1.841464964	0.073369453	-4.049807902	85.58492083
x*	12.82886011	3.053925406	4.200777164	0.00015495	6.646511122	19.01120909

When reporting results, be sure to note the appropriate units of measure for both food expenditures and weekly income. For example, the results above suggest that when weekly income increases by $100, food expenditures increase by $12.83.

6.3.2 Changing the Scale of y

The dependent variable can be transformed, or scaled, using a similar process as above. To change food expenditures to be reported in cents instead of dollars,

- Create a column labeled y^*.
- In the first empty cell of this column, type **=A2*100**.
- Copy this formula down the column.
- Use y^* as the dependent variable in the regression. Results are

	Coefficients	Standard Error	t Stat	P-value	Lower 95%	Upper 95%
Intercept	4076.755647	2213.865442	1.841464964	0.073369453	-404.9807902	8558.492083
Income	12.82886011	3.053925406	4.200777164	0.00015495	6.646511122	19.01120909

These results say that when weekly income increases by $1, food expenditures increase by 12.83 cents.

6.3.3 Formulas for Scaling Data

Any (appropriate!) scaling of the data can be performed as above. The most frequently used mathematical operators in Excel are

/ division	Example: **=A2/16**
* multiplication	Example: **=B2*4**
^ raising to a power	Example: **=B2^2**

As always, take care in *correctly* and *specifically* reporting your results!

6.4 Choosing a Functional Form

If it is determined that the linear specification of the model is not appropriate, transforming the original data is easily done in Excel. Deciding whether or not the linear specification is appropriate is a bit more difficult, as is deciding on the appropriate functional form. With some work, however, Excel can help in deciding on a functional form.

6.4.1 Transforming the Original Data

Using combinations of the natural log and reciprocal transformations leads to many common functional forms, so these two transformations are discussed here.

- Return to the worksheet containing the original data.

The Reciprocal Model, $y_t = \beta_1 + \beta_2 \dfrac{1}{x_t} + e_t$

- Create a new column called **1/x**. In the first empty cell of this column, type **=1/B2**, where B2 contains the first (original) observation on weekly income. Copy the formula down the column.

- Perform a regression as usual, using the column **1/x** as the dependent variable (the X-range).

The Log-Log Model, $\ln y_t = \beta_1 + \beta_2 \ln x_t + e$

- Create two columns, **lny** and **lnx**.
- In the column **lny**, calculate the natural log of food expenditures by typing =ln(A2) in the first empty cell. Copy the formula down the column.
- Do the same for food expenditures; in the first empty cell of column **lnx**, type =ln(B2) and copy the formula down the column.
- Perform a regression, choosing the new data columns, **lny** and **lnx** as the Y-Range and X-Range, respectively.

Other Models

The Log-Linear (Exponential), Linear-Log, and Log-Inverse models can be defined using combinations of the log and reciprocal transformations. The interpretation of results will be specific to the particular model used. For example, for the Log-Log specification, a portion of the regression output is

	Coefficients	Standard Error	t Stat	P-value
Intercept	0.299762103	0.895384575	0.334785869	0.73962763
lnx	0.694044986	0.137490911	5.047933561	1.14292E-05

The estimate b_2=.694 is interpreted as the price elasticity of demand for food. When weekly income increases by 1%, food expenditures increase by .694%. The Log-Log model is often referred to as the Constant Elasticity model, since the estimate of elasticity does not change over the pertinent range.

6.4.2 Useful Graphs

Choosing how to transform the data is based on the decision about the best functional form to represent the relationship between y and x. While there are no set "rules" for choosing the right functional form, several "guides" can be used for decision-making purposes.

Plotting y Against x

- To prepare to plot the data, from the worksheet containing the original data, move the column containing the food expenditures to the right of the column of weekly expenditures. Do this by clicking on the column letter A. Place the cursor over the edge of the highlighted section until it changes from a cross to an arrow. Left click, hold down, and drag the column to the right. Release, and the data are now in the new column.

	A	B	C	D
1	Y=Food Ex	X=Weekly Income		
2	52.25	258.3		
3	58.32	343.1		
4	81.79	425		
5	119.9	467.5		
6	125.8	482.9		
7	100.46	487.7		
8	121.51	496.5		
9	100.08	519.4		
10	127.75	543.3		

	A	B	C	D
1		X=Weekly	Y=Food Expenditu	
2		258.3	52.25	
3		343.1	58.32	
4		425	81.79	
5		467.5	119.9	
6		482.9	125.8	
7		487.7	100.46	
8		496.5	121.51	

Note: Whatever appears in the first column will be placed on the horizontal axis of a scatter plot graph in Excel.

- From the menu bar, choose **Insert/Chart**. Alternatively, click on the Chart Wizard icon the toolbar.

- Under the Standard Types tab, choose **XY (Scatter)** chart type.

- Choose the desired **Chart Sub-type** as the first (default) option.

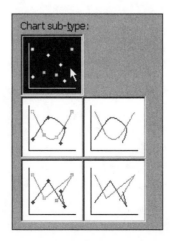

- Click **Next** .
- To fill in the Data range, click on the box with the red arrow and highlight both columns, *x* and *y*, including labels. Hit Enter or click again on the red arrow. A picture of the graph appears above the data range box.

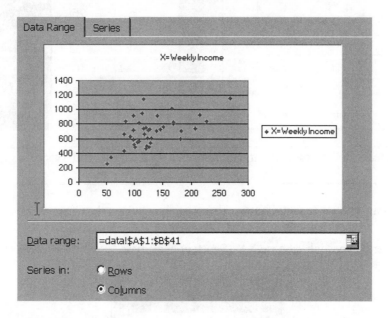

- Click **Next** .
- The Chart Options dialog box appears, opened to the Titles tab. You may specify details of the graph now, or   change settings later. Label the graph "Food Expenditures and Weekly Income" in the **Chart Title:** box.
- Label the x-axis "Weekly Income".
- Label the y-axis "Food Expenditures".

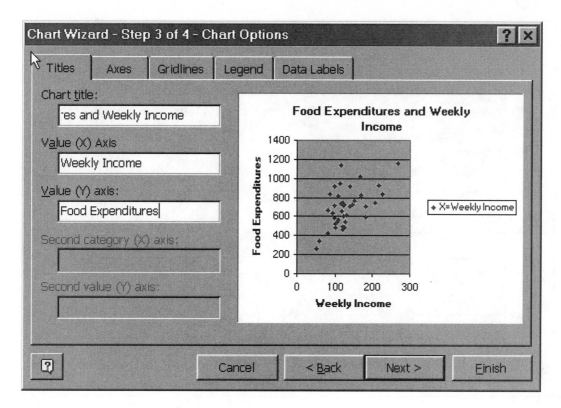

- Click on the Legends tab.
- Click the Show Legend box so the check disappears.
- Click **Next** . (The Axes, Gridlines, and Data Labels can be formatted later, if desired).
- The Place Chart: box appears. Place the graph on a new worksheet named "Y and X graph".

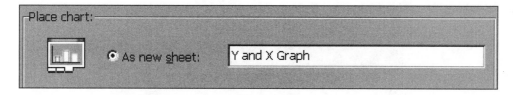

- Click **Finish**. The graph appears on the newly created worksheet.

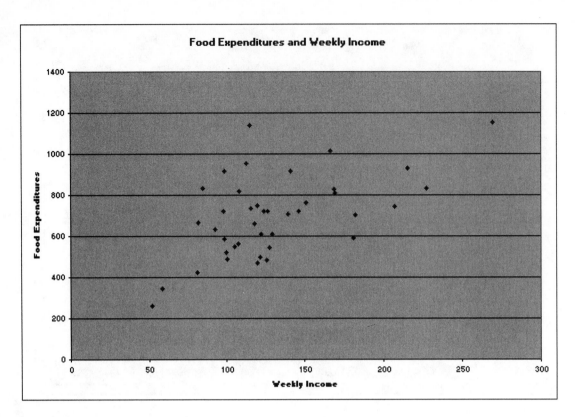

Looking at the plot of the data, it isn't exactly clear if the relationship is linear or not. Examining a graph of the residuals may help.

- Run a regression, and under Output options, choose **Residual Plots**.

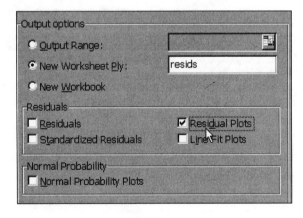

Along with the regression output, a graph of the estimated errors, or residuals, is produced. The graph will need formatting.

- Click on the chart. Resize the chart and rename the axes and title.

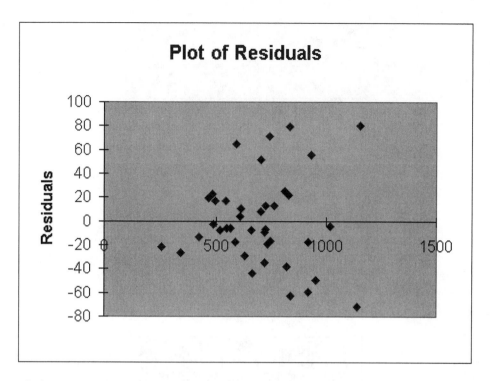

From this graph, it appears the residuals are scattered around zero, but it is difficult to see if there is a concentration of positive or negative values in any certain area. A bar chart might show any concentrations better.

- **Right click** anywhere on the chart.
- Choose **Chart Type**.

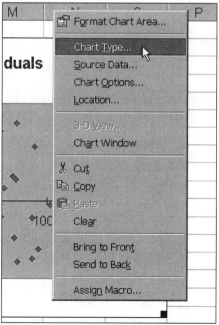

- Choose **Chart Type: Column**.

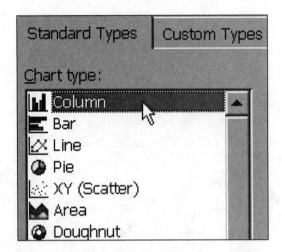

- Click **OK**. The graph is converted to a bar chart, which again, needs some formatting.
- Left click on the horizontal axis so that small boxes appear at each end.
- Right click the axis and choose **Format Axis**.

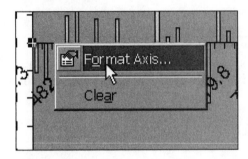

- Set Tick Mark Labels to **None**.

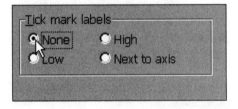

- Click **OK**. The graph no longer has axis values and the bars are clearly seen.

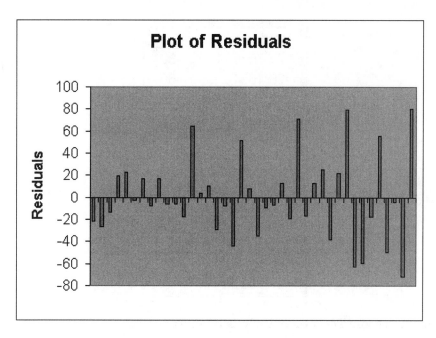

This chart shows the occurrences of the residuals much better. Now, we see there does not appear to be a concentration of either positive or negative values. Do note, however, that the "bars" at the right seem to be taller than the ones on the left. This residual pattern will be discussed in Chapter 12.

> **Note**: While looking at plots of the original variables and of the regression residuals is helpful, there are no easy rules for deciding which functional form to use. You, the econometrician, must make that call based on knowledge and experience.

6.5 Testing for Normality

When choosing the functional form for a particular model, we want to ensure that the resulting errors are normally distributed. Hypothesis testing and interval estimation are based on this assumption. A histogram of the residuals can suggest the distribution of the errors, and the Jarque-Bera test statistic can be used to formally test for normality.

6.5.1 Creating a Histogram of the Residuals

- If not done previously, run a regression of the food expenditures model, choosing the **Residuals** output option.

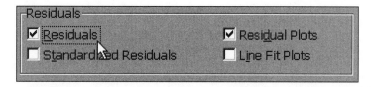

- Examine the values of the residuals, noting the lowest and highest values.
- Create a BIN column next to the residuals column. The Bin values will determine the category values for the histogram. In this column, enter the values -80, -60, -40, -20, 0, 20, 40, 60, and 80.

Residuals	Bin
-21.6545	-80
-26.4634	-60
-13.5002	-40
19.15752	-20
23.08188	0
-2.87391	20
17.04715	40
-7.32066	60
17.28325	80
-6.21951	✚
-5.7193	
-17.7597	

- From the menu bar, choose **Tools/Data Analysis/Histogram**. Click **OK**.

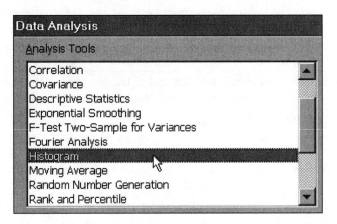

- For the Input Range, highlight the residuals, including label.
- For the Bin Range, highlight the values created in the Bin column, including labels.
- Check the **Labels** box.
- Place the output on a new worksheet called Histo.
- Check the **Chart Output** box.
- Click **OK**.

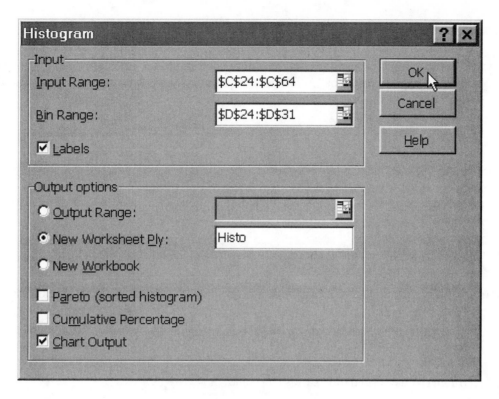

- The Bin values and Frequencies appear, along with the histogram. Format the histogram graph as needed. (Remove legend, resize, rename title, etc).

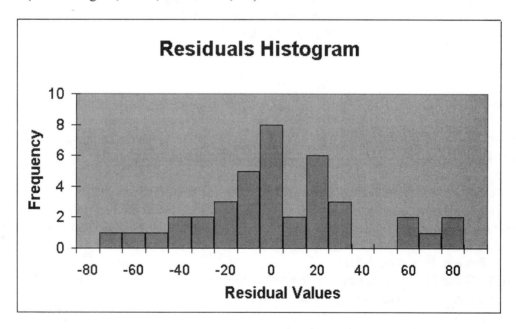

The residuals seem to be centered around zero, but the symmetry of the distribution seems questionable. A formal test of normality, the Jarque-Bera test, uses skewness and kurtosis, which can be easily estimated with Excel.

6.5.2 Skewness and Kurtosis

Excel has a tool called **Descriptive Statistics**, which can be found on the **Tools/Data Analysis** menu. You are encouraged to explore this tool. While it is a quick and easy way to obtain statistics about our residuals, we will compute skewness and kurtosis directly.

Skewness is a measure of asymmetry of a distribution about its mean. For a sample $x_1, x_2, \ldots, x_T$ an empirical measure of skewness is $S = \dfrac{\sum(x_i - \bar{x})^3 / T}{\sigma_x^3}$, where $\sigma_x = \sqrt{\dfrac{1}{T}\sum_{i=1}^{T}(x_i - \bar{x})^2}$.

Kurtosis measures the peakedness, or flatness, of a distribution. An empirical measure of Kurtosis is

$$K = \frac{\sum(x_i - \bar{x})^4 / T}{\sigma_x^4}$$

In the case of the least squares residuals, $\hat{e}$, the formulas simplify because $\sum_{i=1}^{T}\hat{e}_i = 0$, making $\bar{\hat{e}} = 0$. Thus the formulas for skewness and kurtosis of the least squares residuals are $S = \dfrac{\sum\hat{e}_i^3 / T}{\tilde{\sigma}^3}$, where

$\tilde{\sigma} = \sqrt{\dfrac{1}{T}\sum_{i=1}^{T}\hat{e}_i^2}$. Similarly, the formula for kurtosis becomes $K = \dfrac{\sum\hat{e}_i^4 / T}{\tilde{\sigma}^4}$

Skewness measures the symmetry of the data, a value of zero indicating perfect symmetry. Kurtosis refers to the "peakedness" of the distribution, with a value of 3 for a normal distribution. Using these measures, the test statistic for the Jarque-Bera test for normality is

$$JB = \frac{T}{6}\left(S^2 + \frac{(K-3)^2}{4}\right)$$

where S is skewness and K is kurtosis. This test statistic follows a chi-square distribution with 2 degrees of freedom. We will now calculate this value for the food expenditures model.

- Return to the worksheet containing the regression results and the residuals.
- Copy the column containing the least squares residuals to a new worksheet in A1:41.
- In the column to the right of the label Residuals, type the labels **ehat2**, **ehat3** and **ehat4**. In the first empty cell below the label **ehat2**, B2, type **=A2^2** where A2 contains the first residual.
- Copy the formula down the column.
- In columns C and D, create the residuals to the third and fouth powers, respectively.
- Now you are in a position to compute the S, K and JB statistics

With formulas showing, this portion of the worksheet should look like

	A	B	C	D	E	F
1	Residuals	ehat2	ehat3	ehat4	test for normality	
2	-21.6545021173561	=A2^2	=A2^3	=A2^4	sigtilde2	=SUM(B2:B41)/40
3	-26.4633754865811	=A3^2	=A3^3	=A3^4	sigtilde	=SQRT(F2)
4	-13.5002119127547	=A4^2	=A4^3	=A4^4	skewness	=SUM(C2:C41)/(40*F3^3)
5	19.1575225425276	=A5^2	=A5^3	=A5^4	kurtosis	=SUM(D2:D41)/(40*F3^4)
6	23.0818780863241	=A6^2	=A6^3	=A6^4	JB	=(40/6)*(F4^2 +((F5-3)^2)/4)
7	-2.87390719872641	=A7^2	=A7^3	=A7^4	p-value	=CHIDIST(F6,2)

The values will be

test for normality	
sigtilde2	1357.783286
sigtilde	36.84811103
skewness	0.396919923
kurtosis	2.874150903
JB	1.076699494
p-value	0.583710735

- To calculate the chi-square critical value for a 5% test, in an empty cell type

=CHIINV(0.05,2)

where .05 is alpha, and 2 is the degrees of freedom. The result is **5.991476**. The *JB* test statistic is below the critical value, so we fail to reject the null hypothesis that the residuals are distributed normally.

- To calculate the *p*-value associated with the *JB* statistic, in an empty cell type

=CHIDIST(F6,2)

where **F6** contains the JB test statistic. The resulting *p*-value is **0.534147**. Comparing this to a critical value of .05, we, again, fail to reject the null hypothesis of normality.

Chapter 7 The Multiple Regression Model

Now that you are an expert in using Excel for the simple linear regression model, transition to the multiple regression model is easy. Instead of only one explanatory variable in the model, more than one can be used and more realistic models can be estimated.

7.1 Least Squares Estimation of the Multivariate Model

7.1.1 Estimation of the Model Parameters

Using Excel to perform multivariate regression is just like estimating the simple model, except we will include all explanatory variables of interest.

- Open the file *table7-1.dat*. The Import Wizard dialog box appears.
- Remember to choose **Fixed Width** under the Original Data Type option.

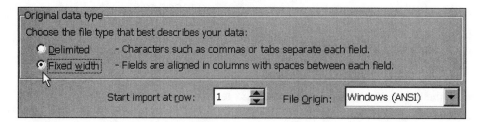

- Click **Next**, then **Finish**.
- Immediately save the file as an Excel file, say *hamburg.xls*. The first column is total weekly revenue (in thousands of dollars), the next column contains a measure of average price of the product (in dollars), and the third column contains weekly advertising expenditures (in thousands of dollars).
- Add a row to the beginning of the file and type labels for each column. (*tr*, *p*, and *a*). (Highlight the row number 1. Choose **Insert/Rows**.)

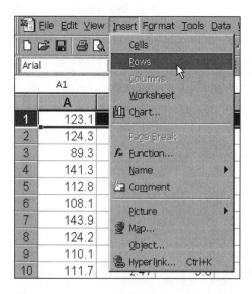

- Choose **Tools/Data Analysis/Regression**, and the dialog box appears.
- Specify *tr* as the **Y-Range**.

- Specify <u>both</u> columns, *p* and *a*, as the **X-range** by highlighting from B1 to C52.
- Check the **Labels** box.
- Choose to have the output placed on a new worksheet named "reg".
- Check the <u>**Residuals**</u> option. Do <u>***NOT***</u> choose **Line Fit Plots**. The graphs produced by this option are not appropriate in the multivariate context.

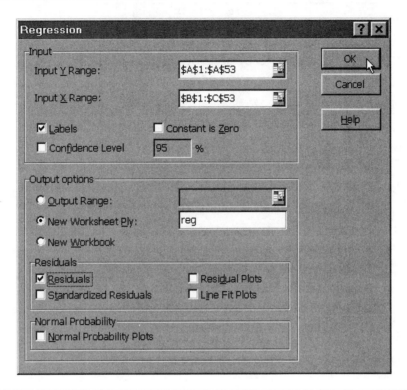

Note the range specified for the X-Range. It begins with the first observation on price and ends with the last observation on advertising expenditures.

- Click **OK**. The regression results appear on the worksheet named "reg" and needs to be formatted as usual.

The results look very similar to what we've seen before, except now we have parameter estimates and other information on *p* AND *a*. This portion of the output appears as

	Coefficients	Standard Error	t Stat	P-value	Lower 95%	Upper 95%
Intercept	104.785514	6.482718984	16.1638217	2.83516E-21	91.75800996	117.8130172
p	-6.6419301	3.191192928	-2.0813314	0.042650528	-13.05486847	-0.228991673
a	2.98429895	0.166936136	17.8768901	4.11139E-23	2.648828431	3.319769475

7.1.2 Estimation of σ^2

The estimated variance of the model can be found in the regression output just as it was in Chapter 3. Although it is not directly reported as such, the MS Residual from the ANOVA table is an estimate of the model variance. Also, the Standard Error reported in the Summary Output is the square root of the estimated variance. From the regression output, these results are

	A	B	C	D
1	SUMMARY OUTPUT			
2				
3	*Regression Statistics*			
4	Multiple R	0.933372225		
5	R Square	0.87118371		
6	Adjusted R Square	0.865816364		
7	Standard Error	6.026483189	← This equals $\sqrt{\hat{\sigma}^2}$.	
8	Observations	51		
9				
10	ANOVA			
11		*df*	*SS*	*MS*
12	Regression	2	11789.84496	5894.922479
13	Residual	48	1743.287982	36.31849963
14	Total	50	13533.13294	↑ This equals $\hat{\sigma}^2$.

7.2 Sampling Properties of the LS Estimators

7.2.1 Estimated Variances of the LS Estimators

The regression output provides standard errors for the b_1, b_2, and b_3. If we square these values, we have estimates of the estimators' variances.

16		Coefficients	Standard Error	t Stat	P-value
17	Intercept	104.7855136	6.482718984	16.16382167	2.83516E-21
18	p	-6.641930069	3.191192928	-2.081331407	0.042650528
19	a	2.984298953	0.166936136	17.87689007	4.11139E-23

- In cell C20, type =**C17^2**.
- Copy this formula into cells C21 and C22.

The resulting estimated variances are

var(b1)	42.02564543
var(b2)	10.18371231
var(b3)	0.027867674

Excel does not compute the covariance matrix for the LS estimators.

7.2.2 Testing the Assumption of Normally Distributed Errors

If we can assume that the errors of the model are normally distributed, we can then assume that the dependent variable, y_t, is normally distributed. Since the LS estimators are linear functions of the dependent variable, the LS estimators are therefore distributed normally. The inferences we make about the unknown parameters, (confidence intervals and hypothesis testing) rely on this assumption. So, let us test whether the errors are normal, using the Jarque-Bera test presented in Chapter 6. Following the steps on page 54 of this manual, you will produce a page with the following formulas.

	A	B	C	D	E	F
1	Residuals	ehat2	ehat3	ehat4	test for normality	
2	-5.93831487868454	=A2^2	=A2^3	=A2^4	sigtilde2	=SUM(B2:B53)/52
3	4.25007641955038	=A3^2	=A3^3	=A3^4	sigtilde	=SQRT(F2)
4	-11.5558078666284	=A4^2	=A4^3	=A4^4	skewness	=SUM(C2:C53)/(52*F3^3)
5	6.48960337061652	=A5^2	=A5^3	=A5^4	kurtosis	=SUM(D2:D53)/(52*F3^4)
6	9.19281769067486	=A6^2	=A6^3	=A6^4	JB	=(52/6)*(F4^2 +((F5-3)^2)/4)
7	8.23773989683625	=A7^2	=A7^3	=A7^4	p-value	=CHIDIST(F6,2)

The results are:

test for normality	
sigtilde2	34.71477751
sigtilde	5.891924771
skewness	-0.045982527
kurtosis	1.890079441
JB	2.687492641
p-value	0.260866546

The value of the JB statistic is 2.68 which is less than the .05 critical value from a $\chi^2_{(2)}$ distribution, 5.99, so the null hypothesis that the errors are distributed normally is not rejected. We make the same decision based on the p-value = .261 > alpha = .05.

The assumption of normality is met and we can continue with inference in the multivariate model.

7.3 Inference in the Multivariate Regression Model

Having met the assumption of normality, we can now proceed with interval estimation and hypothesis testing based on the t-distribution.

7.3.1 Interval Estimation

The 95% confidence interval for each parameter is provided by default in the Excel regression output. To have a different confidence level reported, specify the Confidence Level in the regression dialog box.

- Return to the worksheet containing the original data.
- Run a regression using **Tools/Data Analysis/Regression**.

- Check the **Confidence Level** box and set the level to 98.
- Set all other desired options.
- Click **OK**.

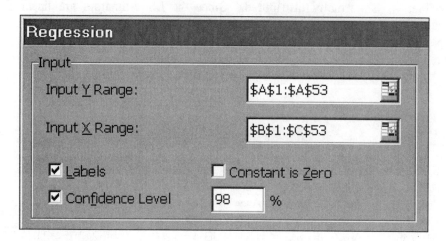

Both the 95% and 98% confidence intervals are reported for the β_1, β_2, and β_3.

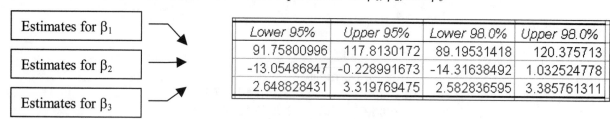

Lower 95%	Upper 95%	Lower 98.0%	Upper 98.0%
91.75800996	117.8130172	89.19531418	120.375713
-13.05486847	-0.228991673	-14.31638492	1.032524778
2.648828431	3.319769475	2.582836595	3.385761311

The 98% confidence interval for β_3 suggests that an additional $1000 in advertising expenditures leads to an increase in total revenue that is between $2583 and $3386. The 98% confidence interval for β_2 is very wide and goes from negative to positive. The value of zero lies in the interval, which suggests we should formally test the significance of the parameters.

7.3.2 Hypothesis Testing the Significance of a Single Coefficient

Using the t-stats and p-values that are reported in the regression output is the simplest way to test the significance of a single coefficient. The results are

16		Coefficients	Standard Error	t Stat	P-value
17	Intercept	104.7855136	6.482718984	16.16382167	2.83516E-21
18	p	-6.641930069	3.191192928	-2.081331407	0.042650528
19	a	2.984298953	0.166936136	17.87689007	4.11139E-23

Recall that the t-stat is the coefficient divided by its standard error. Based on the reported p-values, b_2 is significant at the 5% level, but not at the 1% level. This result is consistent with the wide confidence interval we calculated for β_2. The standard error for b_2 is relatively "large", causing both the wide interval estimate and the insignificance at the 1% level.

b_3 is significant at virtually any level.

7.3.3 General Hypothesis Testing of a Single Coefficient

In Chapter Five, we developed a template for performing *t*-tests. We can now use this template again to perform general tests about our parameters.

To test for elastic demand, the null and alternative hypotheses are

H_0: $\beta_2 \geq 0$: a decrease in price leads to a decrease in total revenue (demand is price inelastic)
H_1: $\beta_2 < 0$: a decrease in price leads to an increase in total revenue (demand is price elastic)

- Open the file containing the template for *t*- tests that you create in Chapter Five. (See Section 5.3.4 if you need to create it).
- Fill in the required user input, using the results from the regression.

	A	B
1	Hypothesis Testing Using the t-Distribution	
2	**Data Input**	
3	Sample size	52
4	Estimate Value	-6.642
5	StdError	3.191
6	Ho	0
7	Alpha	0.05
8	**Computed Values**	
9	df	50
10	t	-2.08147916
11	**Left-Tailed Test**	
12	Left Critical Value	-1.675905423
13	Decision	Reject Ho
14	p-value	0.021265123
15	**Right-Tailed Test**	
16	Right Critical Value	1.675905423
17	Decision	Fail to Reject Ho
18	p-value	0.978734877
19	**Two-Tailed Test**	
20	Absolute Critical Value	2.008559932
21	Decision	Reject Ho
22	p-value	0.042530246

These are the relevant results, given the H_1

We reject the null hypothesis and conclude that there is sufficient evidence to show that demand is price elastic.

Note: While it may seem as if this test is the same as the test for significance, take care! When we reject this particular null hypothesis, we conclude that demand is price elastic. In the test for significance, we conclude that β_2 is statistically different from zero, indicating that price is "important" in the model. While the numbers we use for these tests may be the same, the tests are different!

To test whether an increase in advertising expenditures is "worth it", that is, total revenues increase enough to cover the increased cost of the advertising, we test

$H_0: \beta_3 \leq 1$
$H_1: \beta_3 > 1$

If the null hypothesis is true, it suggests that a dollar increase in advertising expenditures leads to less than a dollar increase in total revenue. In this case, it doesn't make sense to spend that extra dollar.

- Return to the *t*-test template and redefine the user input consistent with this test.

1	Hypothesis Testing Using the t-Distribution	
2	**Data Input**	
3	Sample size	52
4	Estimate Value	2.984
5	StdError	0.1669
6	Ho	1
7	Alpha	0.05
8	**Computed Values**	
9	df	50
10	t	11.8873577
11	**Left-Tailed Test**	
12	Left Critical Value	-1.675905423
13	Decision	Fail to Reject Ho
14	p-value	1
15	**Right-Tailed Test**	
16	Right Critical Value	1.675905423
17	Decision	Reject Ho
18	p-value	1.74976E-16
19	**Two-Tailed Test**	
20	Absolute Critical Value	2.008559932
21	Decision	Reject Ho
22	p-value	3.49951E-16

These are the relevant results, given the H_1 above.

Again, we reject the null hypothesis and conclude that there is sufficient statistical evidence to suggest that an increase in advertising expenditures is "worth it" in terms of the increase in total revenue.

7.4   *Goodness of Fit and R^2*

The coefficient of determination (R^2) and the ANOVA table are reported for the multivariate regression model as they were for the simple model. And while the interpretation for R^2 is the same, you should be careful when using it as a measure of "goodness of fit". The results from the regression are

✛	A	B	C	D	E	F
1	SUMMARY OUTPUT					
2						
3	*Regression Statistics*					
4	Multiple R	0.93117387				
5	R Square	0.86708478				
6	Adjusted R Square	0.86165967				
7	Standard Error	6.06961054				
8	Observations	52				
9						
10	ANOVA					
11		*df*	*SS*	*MS*	*F*	*Significance F*
12	Regression	2	11776.18388	5888.09194	159.828025	3.36962E-22
13	Residual	49	1805.16843	36.840172		
14	Total	51	13581.35231			

$R^2 = .867$ meaning that 86.7% of the total variation in total revenue is explained by price and advertising expenditures. However, there can be a problem with this measure in the multivariate model. It can be "forced" higher by including more and more explanatory variables, even if they have no economic basis for appearing in the model.

An alternative measure is Adjusted R Square reported just below R Square. This measure adjusts for the number of explanatory variables, so cannot be made larger as R^2 can. The Adjusted-R^2 can also be calculated from the ANOVA table.

$$\bar{R}^2 = 1 - \frac{SSE/(T-K)}{SST/(T-1)} = 1 - \frac{1805.17/49}{13581.35/51} = 0.8617$$

While this solves the problem associated with R^2 (which has a particular interpretation!), the adjusted-R^2 has no interpretation! It is no longer the percent of the variation in total revenue that is explained by the model. It should NOT be used as a device for selecting appropriate explanatory variables; good economic theory should determine the model.

Chapter 8 Further Inference in the Multiple Regression Model

In the last chapter, we used the *t*-test to make inferences about our parameters. In this chapter, we will further examine the multivariate regression model. We will develop a procedure to test multiple hypotheses about our parameters. We will also incorporate non-sample information into our models and develop a test for whether our model specification is appropriate. Finally, we will go in search of collinearity, which can cause problems for regression estimation.

8.1 The F-test

The *t*-test is used to test a specific null hypothesis, such as a single test of significance. With the multiple regression model, we might be interested in testing whether two or more explanatory variables are *jointly* important to the model. The *F*-test allows for testing joint hypotheses, and is based on a comparison of the sum of the squared errors from an unrestricted (full, or "original") model to the sum of squared errors from a model where the null hypothesis has been imposed. This latter model is referred to as the restricted model. The *F*-statistic we will use is

$$F = \frac{(SSE_R - SSE_U)/J}{SSE_U/(T-K)}$$

where

SSE_R and SSE_U are the sum squared errors from the ANOVA tables of the restricted and unrestricted models, respectively. J is the number of hypotheses in the null hypothesis. T is the sample size of the unrestricted model, and K is the number of parameters in the unrestricted model. If the null hypothesis is true, this test statistic follows the *F*-distribution with J numerator and $T-K$ denominator degrees of freedom.

8.1.1 Creating an F-test Template

- Open a blank worksheet in Excel. **Save As** *ftesttemplate.xls*.
- Type a heading such as "Hypothesis Testing Using the *F*-Distribution" in cell A1.
- Type **Data Input** labels and **Computed Values** labels in column A as shown below.
- For appearances, left justify and set to bold font the labels **Data Input** and **Computed Values**.
- Right justify the sub-labels as shown below.

	A
1	Hypothesis Testing Using the F-Distribution
2	**Data Input**
3	J
4	T
5	K
6	SSE-Restricted
7	SSE-Unrestricted
8	Alpha
9	**Computed Values**
10	df-numerator
11	df-denominator
12	F
13	Right Critical Value
14	Decision
15	p-value

In column B, we will type the formulas necessary to calculate the F-statistic, the appropriate decision, and the p-value associated with the calculated F-statistic. The commands are similar to those used to create the t-test template in chapter 5. To calculate the F-statistic for a particular test, see the formula in cell B12. The functions FINV and FDIST are used to find the F-critical value and the p-value associated with the calculated F-statistic, respectively. The syntax of these functions are **FINV(α,df1,df2)** and **FDIST(F-stat,df1,df2)**

- Create the formulas as shown below.

	A	B
1	Hypothesis Testing Using the F-Distribution	
2	**Data Input**	
3	J	
4	T	
5	K	
6	SSE-Restricted	
7	SSE-Unrestricted	
8	Alpha	
9	**Computed Values**	
10	df-numerator	=B3
11	df-denominator	=B4-B5
12	F	=((B6-B7)/B10)/((B7)/B11)
13	Right Critical Value	=FINV(B8,B10,B11)
14	Decision	=IF(B12>B13,"Reject Ho","Fail to Reject Ho")
15	p-value	=FDIST(B12,B10,B11)

- Save this template. It can be used over and over again when performing any F-test!

8.1.2 Performing an F-test

To obtain the information needed in the **Data Input** section of the template, we must run regressions on an unrestricted model and a restricted model. From these, we will use the SSE's from the ANOVA tables. The other regression output is not important at this point.

Let's use the hamburger chain's total revenue example used in chapter seven to test whether price has an effect on total revenue against the alternative that it does not; $H_0:\beta_2=0$ against $H_1: \beta_2\neq0$. The unrestricted model is $tr_t = \beta_1 + \beta_2 p_t + \beta_3 a_t + e_t$. The restricted model takes the null hypothesis as true and is $tr_t = \beta_1 + \beta_3 a_t + e_t$.

- Open the worksheet *hamburg.xls*.
- If you had not done so in chapter seven, run a regression on the full, unrestricted model. (Remember? **Tools/Data Analysis/Regression**). Include both *p* and *a* as explanatory variables.
- Place the results on a new worksheet called *reg*.

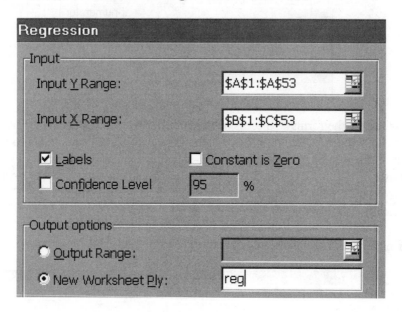

- Click **OK**.
- Run another regression, called *reg2*, in which you **only include *a*** as an explanatory variable.

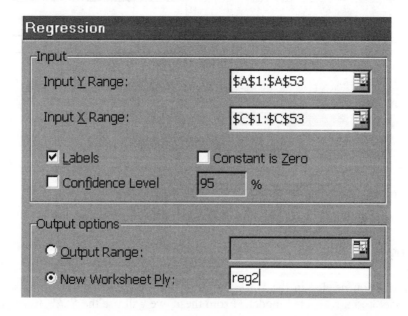

- Click **OK**.

The information you want from these two regressions comes from the ANOVA tables and will be used as the Data Input in the *F*-test template.

- Go to the worksheet *reg*.
- Click on cell C13, which contains the Sum Square Residual.

10	ANOVA					
11		df	SS	MS	F	Significance F
12	Regression	1	11616.59	11616.59	295.62407	1.23585E-22
13	Residual	50	1964.758	39.29516		
14	Total	51	13581.35			

- With cell C13 highlighted, choose **Edit/Copy** from the main menu. A scrolling border appears around the cell.

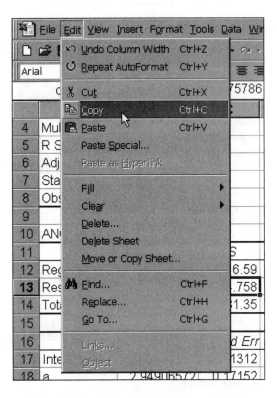

The value is now stored on the Excel's clipboard and be pasted as desired.

An alternative method for copying (and other things) is to right-click a chosen object.

- **Right-click** on the cell C13. Choose **Copy**.

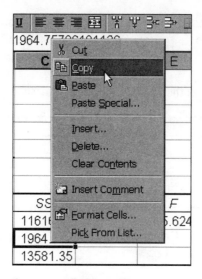

- Open the worksheet *ftesttemplate.xls*, if not already open.
- If this worksheet IS open, go to it by choosing **Window** on the main menu and choosing it.

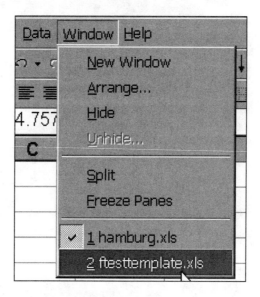

- Highlight cell B7, the unrestricted *SSE*.
- Choose **Edit/Paste** from the menu bar, or
- **Right-click** and choose **Paste**.
- Now repeat this procedure using the restricted *SSE*. Return to *hamburg.xls* and move to the worksheet named *reg2*.
- Highlight the sum squared residual from this restricted model.
- Either choose **Edit/Copy** from the menu or **Right-click** and choose **Copy**.
- Move back to *ftesttemplate.xls* and **Paste** the value in cell B6.
- Type "**1**" in cell B3, since we are testing just one hypothesis.
- Type "**52**" in cell B4 (the sample size).
- Type "**.05**" in cell B5 for testing at the 5% level.

The computed values should now appear, and the appropriate decision reported.

	A	B
1	Hypothesis Testing Using the F-Distribution	
2	**Data Input**	
3	J	1
4	T	52
5	K	3
6	SSE-Restricted	1964.758
7	SSE-Unrestricted	1805.168
8	Alpha	0.05
9	**Computed Values**	
10	df-numerator	1
11	df-denominator	49
12	F	4.331956915
13	Right Critical Value	4.03838385
14	Decision	Reject Ho
15	p-value	0.04265015

Since the F-statistic > F-critical value, and the p-value < alpha, we reject the null hypothesis at the 5% level and conclude the price does have an effect on total revenue.

8.2 Testing the Overall Significance of a Model

Now we consider the case where we want to test the relevance of all the explanatory variables in a multiple regression model. There are $K-1$ explanatory variables and K unknown parameters. We test whether all of the coefficients on the $K-1$ explanatory variables are jointly equal to zero, versus the alternative that at least one of coefficients is not zero.

8.2.1 Using the F-test Template for a Test of Overall Significance

As mentioned earlier, the template you created for F-tests can be used for any F-test of interest. For jointly testing the significance of all of the explanatory variables, we test that all the β's are zero except β_1, the intercept. Using the hamburger chain data, the null and alternative hypotheses are

H_0: $\beta_2 = 0$ and $\beta_3 = 0$
H_1: Either $\beta_2 \neq 0$, $\beta_3 \neq 0$, or both do not equal 0

To find the restricted model, we impose the null hypothesis on the model, which becomes

$$tr_t = \beta_1 + e_t$$

Note that there are **NO** explanatory variables in the model other than the intercept. It can be shown that *in this one case*, the SSE_R is equal to the SST from the unrestricted model. The F-statistic becomes

$$F = \frac{(SST - SSE)/(K-1)}{SSE/(T-K)}$$

All other elements of the F-test are as before. So let's perform a test of overall significance.
- Have both *hamburg.xls* and *ftesttemplate.xls* open.

- From the ANOVA table of the unrestricted model, copy the *SST* in cell **C14** to cell **B6** of the *F*-test template.
- Copy the *SSE* from the ANOVA table, in cell **C13**, to cell **B7** of the *F*-test template.
- The value of *J* is equal to $K-1$, the number of explanatory variables. Type "**2**" in cell B3.
- Set the value of *T* to 52.
- Set the value of *K* to 3.

The results and appropriate decision are

	A	B
1	Hypothesis Testing Using the F-Distribution	
2	**Data Input**	
3	J	2
4	T	52
5	K	3
6	SSE-Restricted	13581.35
7	SSE-Unrestricted	1805.168
8	Alpha	0.05
9	**Computed Values**	
10	df-numerator	2
11	df-denominator	49
12	F	159.8280376
13	Right Critical Value	3.186585218
14	Decision	Reject Ho
15	p-value	3.36961E-22

We reject the null hypothesis and conclude that our model is significant at the 5% level; price or advertising expenditures, or both have a significance effect on total revenue.

8.2.2 Using the Regression Output to Test for Overall Significance of the Model

Now that you have worked through this *F*-test of model significance, you will understand some of the regression output provided by Excel's ANOVA table not previously explained. *F* and *Significance F* are the last two entries in the ANOVA output and are just what you might suspect they are. *F* is the calculated *F*-test statistic and *Significance F* is the associated *p*-value.

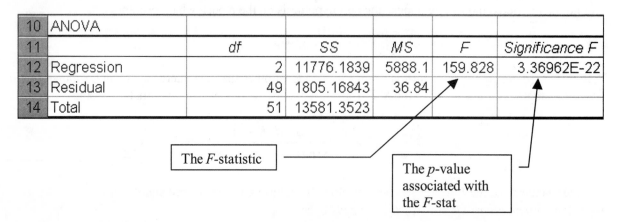

10	ANOVA					
11		*df*	*SS*	*MS*	*F*	*Significance F*
12	Regression	2	11776.1839	5888.1	159.828	3.36962E-22
13	Residual	49	1805.16843	36.84		
14	Total	51	13581.3523			

The *F*-statistic

The *p*-value associated with the *F*-stat

If we compare the *F*-statistic to a critical value, or more easily, compare the p-value to alpha, we reject the null hypothesis and conclude the model is statistically "important".

8.3 An Extended Model

The concept of diminishing marginal returns is an important one in economics, and you should carefully consider this when modeling economic relationships. In our total revenue model, it seems reasonable that each and every dollar increase in advertising expenditures would not lead to the same increase in total revenue; that is, the possibility of diminishing marginal returns to advertising should be considered. To allow for this possibility, we include the explanatory variable squared in the model.

$$tr_t = \beta_1 + \beta_2 p_t + \beta_3 a_t + \beta_4 a^2 + e_t$$

- Return to the worksheet containing the original data in the workbook *hamburg.xls*.
- Label column D "a2".
- In cell D2, type the formula **=C2^2**.
- Copy this formula down the column.
- From the main menu, choose **Tools/Data Analysis/Regression**.
- Choose the *tr* data for the **Y-Range**.
- Include *p*, *a*, and *a2* in the **X-Range**.
- Include labels and check the **Labels** box.
- Place the output on a new worksheet named "dimreg1".
- Click **OK**.

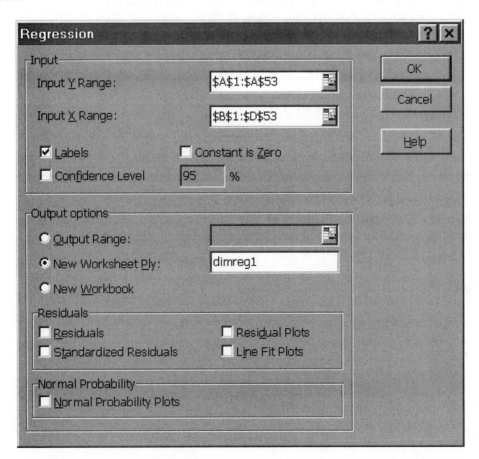

A portion of the regression output is shown here. Not shown are the *F*-statistic and associated *p*-value. But from the full regression output, we see that the model is significant.

16		Coefficients	Standard Error	t Stat	P-value
17	Intercept	104.8146701	6.577833458	15.9345278	8.46813E-21
18	p	-6.581742032	3.459314579	-1.902614487	0.063099015
19	a	2.947464896	0.785496021	3.752361333	0.000472373
20	a2	0.001732619	0.036086747	0.048012603	0.961905417

Price is now insignificant at the 5% level when squared advertising expenditures are included in the model.

The estimated coefficient on a^2 is positive, not as expected, and comparing the *p*-value to (any level of) alpha, we conclude that it is not significantly different from zero. This suggests that there are no diminishing returns to advertising, which goes against our theory. The high standard error for a^2 indicates imprecise estimation. One way to increase precision is to increase our sample size. Let us, then, do that and see if we still find no evidence of diminishing marginal returns.

- Open the data file *chap8-3.dat* containing 78 weekly observations. **Save As** *hamburg2.xls*.
- Insert a row at the top of the data.
- Label the columns *tr*, *p*, and *a*, respectively.
- Create the new column, *a2*, containing the squared advertising expenditures.
- Run a multiple regression on these data, including all 78 observations.

The new results are

16		Coefficients	Standard Error	t Stat	P-value
17	Intercept	110.464124	3.741410173	29.52472969	1.10053E-42
18	p	-10.19791678	1.581821866	-6.44694387	1.0364E-08
19	a	3.360998695	0.421708034	7.969966002	1.47623E-11
20	a2	-0.02675498	0.015887366	-1.684041252	0.09638765

By increasing our sample size, we have increased the precision of our estimators. Price is now significant. Advertising expenditures squared is now negative, as expected, and performing a one-tailed *t*-test shows that it is significant at the 5% level. (Recall that the *p*-value reported by Excel is for a two-tailed test).

8.4 Testing Some Economic Hypotheses

Using this expanded model for total revenue, we will now examine several hypotheses of interest, using both *t*-tests and *F*-tests.

8.4.1 The Significance of Advertising

In testing whether advertising affects total revenue, we must now consider the significance of both β_3 and β_4. If either one is not zero, then advertising expenditures affect total revenue. The joint null hypothesis is H_0: $\beta_3 = 0$, $\beta_4 = 0$ and the F-test is appropriate. We, again, need to estimate the restricted model in order to get SSE_R. This model is $tr_t = \beta_1 + \beta_2 p_t + e_t$.

- Return to the original data with 78 observations.
- Run a regression using tr as the dependent variable and p as the only explanatory variable.
- Save the output to a worksheet named *restrictreg1*.

The ANOVA results are

10	ANOVA					
11		df	SS	MS	F	Significance F
12	Regression	1	436.9240512	436.9240512	1.588257639	0.211431079
13	Residual	76	20907.33082	275.0964582		
14	Total	77	21344.25487			

- Copy the sum squared residual in cell C13 to the clipboard. (**Right click** and choose **Copy**).
- Open the file *ftesttemplate.xls*, if not already open.
- Place the cursor on cell **B6** of the F-test template.
- **Right click** and choose **Paste**.
- Return to the file *hamburg2.xls* and the worksheet containing the unrestricted model (*dimreg1*).
- Copy the SSE from cell C13 to the F-test template, cell **B7**, the unrestricted SSE.
- Fill in the values $J=2$, $T=78$, and $K=4$ (based on the unrestricted model).

The results are

	A	B
1	Hypothesis Testing Using the F-Distribution	
2	**Data Input**	
3	J	2
4	T	78
5	K	4
6	SSE-Restricted	20907.33082
7	SSE-Unrestricted	2592.300992
8	Alpha	0.05
9	**Computed Values**	
10	df-numerator	2
11	df-denominator	74
12	F	261.4110421
13	Right Critical Value	3.120348424
14	Decision	Reject Ho
15	p-value	2.85307E-34

We reject the null hypothesis and conclude that advertising expenditures do significantly affect total revenue.

8.4.2 Finding the Optimal Level of Advertising Expenditures

An important issue to the owner of this hamburger chain is finding the optimal level of advertising; that is, the revenue maximizing level of advertising. The optimization procedure leads us to conclude that total revenue is maximized at the point where the marginal cost is equal to the marginal benefit of advertising. Taking the derivative of total revenue with respect to advertising expenditures, we find the marginal benefit is

$$\beta_3 + 2\beta_4 a_t$$

Assuming no other costs of increased advertising, we set this equal to \$1. We can then substitute in our estimates for β_3 and β_4 and solve for the optimal level of advertising, $\hat{a}_t$.

$$3.361 + 2(-.0268)\ \hat{a}_t = 1$$

- Place the cursor in an empty cell just below the regression output on the worksheet *dimreg1* from the workbook *hamburg2.xls*.
- Type the formula **=(1–3.361)/(2*–.0268)**. The result is 44.04850746.

Recall that advertising expenditures are reported in thousands of dollars, so the optimal level of advertising seems to be \$44,048.50.

If management thinks this dollar amount is too high, and believes the optimal level is actually \$40,000, we can test this belief. The null hypothesis is H_0: $\beta_3 + 2\beta_4(40) = 1$ against the alternative H_0: $\beta_3 + 2\beta_4(40) \neq 1$.

While a *t*-test could be used to test this single hypothesis, it would require a calculation using the covariance between b_3 and b_4. Since Excel does not report the covariance matrix for the LS estimators, we will instead use the *F*-test. The restricted model in this case becomes

$$tr_t = \beta_1 + \beta_2 p_t + (1-80\beta_4)a_t + e_t$$

Multiplying the third term out and rearranging, we obtain an expression for the model convenient for estimation.

$$(tr_t - a_t) = \beta_1 + \beta_2 p_t + \beta_4(a^2_t - 80a_t) + e_t$$

- Return to the worksheet containing the data for *hamburg2.xls*.
- Highlight column B. Insert a column by choosing **Insert/Columns** from the menu bar.
- Label this new column *tr-a*. In the first empty cell of this column, type **=A2–D2**.
- Copy this formula down the column.
- Highlight column D and insert a new column. Label this *a2-80a*.
- In the first empty cell, type **=F2–(80*E2)**. Copy the formula down the column.
- Choose **Tools/Data Analysis/Regression**.
- Use *tr-a* as the **Y-Range**.
- Use *p* and *a2–80a* as the **X-Range**. Perform this regression as usual.

> **Note:** The reason for inserting columns as we did is because, in Excel, the columns used for the X-Range (the explanatory variables) must be in adjacent columns. If you ever find that you want to run a regression and the explanatory variables are not all in adjacent columns, simply highlight and move things around as needed.

The ANOVA regression results are

10	ANOVA					
11		df	SS	MS	F	Significance F
12	Regression	2	7259.215137	3629.607569	104.9208266	1.84998E-22
13	Residual	75	2594.533196	34.59377594		
14	Total	77	9853.748333			

This sum squared residual can now be used in the *F*-test template. Remember what we are testing? H_0: β_3 + $2\beta_4(40)$ =1 or that $40,000 is the optimal level of advertising expenditures.

- Copy the *SSE* from this restricted model to cell B6 of the *F*-test template.
- Set *J*=1 since we have only a single null hypothesis.
- Fill in the other values for the **Data Input** if needed.

The results from this test are

	A	B
1	Hypothesis Testing Using the F-Distribution	
2	**Data Input**	
3	J	1
4	T	78
5	K	4
6	SSE-Restricted	2594.533196
7	SSE-Unrestricted	2592.300992
8	Alpha	0.05
9	**Computed Values**	
10	df-numerator	1
11	df-denominator	74
12	F	0.063720657
13	Right Critical Value	3.97022859
14	Decision	Fail to Reject Ho
15	p-value	0.801408932

We cannot reject the hypothesis that $40,000 is the optimal level of weekly advertising expenditures at the 5% level.

8.4.3 The Optimal Level of Advertising and Price

Let's say now that management believes that the optimal level of advertising is $40,000 <u>and</u> that with a price of $2.00, total revenue will be $175,000 based on the model

$$E(tr_t) = \beta_1 + \beta_2 p_t + \beta_3 a_t + \beta_4 a^2 + e_t$$

We want to jointly test these two conjectures by testing the null hypotheses H_0: $\beta_3 + 2\beta_4(40)$ =1 and $\beta_1 + 2\beta_2 + 40\beta_3 + 1600\beta_4$ against the alternative that one of these is not true. Since *J*=2, we must perform an *F*-test. The restricted model is found by substituting both the hypotheses in the null on the model and rearranging terms to form a model suitable for estimation. It can be shown that the equation used to estimate the restricted model is

$$(tr_t - a_t - 135) = \beta_2(p_t - 2) + \beta_4(a^2_t - 80a_t + 1000) + e_t$$

- Return to the worksheet containing the original data in *hamburg2.xls*.
- Create three new columns labeled *tr–a–135*, *p–2*, and *a2–80a+1600*.
- In the first empty cell of *tr–a–135*, type the formula **=B2–135**, where cell B2 contains *tr–a*.
- In the first empty cell of *p–2*, type **=C2-2**, where cell C2 contains *p*.
- In the first empty cell of *a2–80a+1600*, type **=F2–(80*E2)+1600**, where cell F2 contains *a2* and E2 contains *a*.
- Highlight the three cells containing these new formulas.
- Place the cursor on the lower right-hand corner of this selection until it turns into a cross-hatch.

G	H	I
tr-a-135	p-2	a2-80a+1600
-24.3	-0.08	761.76

- Left click, hold, and drag down to row 79. Release and the values appear in the cells.
- Run a regression and use *tr–a–135* as the **Y-Range**. Use *p–2*, and *a2–80a+1600* as the **X-Range**. (Remember, we want the *SSE* from this restricted model).
- In the regression dialog box, check the **Constant is Zero** box. (Notice from the model above, there is no intercept).

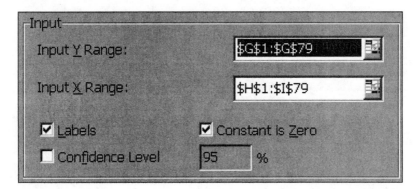

The ANOVA results are

10	ANOVA					
11		df	SS	MS	F	Significance F
12	Regression	2	7138.63	3569.315	99.91016	7.08705E-22
13	Residual	76	2715.119	35.72524		
14	Total	78	9853.748			

- Copy this value of SSE_R to the *F*-test template in cell **B6**.
- Set *J=2*, *T=78*, and *K=4*.

- Be sure the SSE_U is still in cell B7. (If it is not, return to worksheet *dimreg1* in the workbook *hamburg2.xls* to obtain the sum squared residual).

Results for this test are

	A	B
1	Hypothesis Testing Using the F-Distribution	
2	**Data Input**	
3	J	2
4	T	78
5	K	4
6	SSE-Restricted	2715.11854
7	SSE-Unrestricted	2592.300992
8	Alpha	0.05
9	**Computed Values**	
10	df-numerator	2
11	df-denominator	74
12	F	1.752979042
13	Right Critical Value	3.120348424
14	Decision	Fail to Reject Ho
15	p-value	0.18037458

We fail to reject the joint null and conclude that the data are compatible with the hypotheses that the optimal level of advertising is $40,000 per week and that total revenue will be (on average) $175,000 when the price is $2.00.

8.5 The Use of Nonsample Information

Oftentimes we have information about a particular model that does not come directly from the data. The information may come from past experience or from economic tenets, and, if correct, should be used to improve the model. To show how to incorporate nonsample information into a model, we will use a model of demand for beer (q) based on its price (p_B), the price of other liquor (p_L), the price of all other remaining goods and services (p_R), and income (m). The nonsample information is that consumers do not suffer from "money illusion"; that is, when all prices and income go up by the same proportion, there is no change in quantity demanded.

We will use a log-log functional form for the model, and then impose restrictions that incorporate our nonsample information. The unrestricted model is

$$ln(q) = \beta_1 + \beta_2 ln(p_B) + \beta_3 ln(p_L) + \beta_4 ln(p_R) + \beta_5 ln(m) + e$$

and will impose the restriction $\beta_2 + \beta_3 + \beta_4 + \beta_5 = 0$. Rearranging this restriction, we have $\beta_4 = -\beta_2 - \beta_3 - \beta_5$, which can be substituted into the unrestricted model. After some manipulation, the equation we will estimate is

$$ln(q) = \beta_1 + \beta_2 \ln\left(\frac{p_B}{p_R}\right) + \beta_3 \ln\left(\frac{p_L}{p_R}\right) + \beta_5 \ln\left(\frac{m}{p_R}\right) + e$$

This equation incorporates the properties of logarithms, as well as the nonsample information. We will estimate this "restricted" model as usual, but the least squares estimates we get will be "restricted least squares estimates". This procedure is therefore called Restricted Least Squares Estimation.

- Open the data file *table8-3.dat* and **Save As** *beerdemand.xls*. Note that the original data have associated labels already.
- Label the next 3 columns *pb/pr, pl/pr,* and *m/pr*.
- For *pb/pr*, in cell F2, type **=B2/$D$2**. The $ "anchors" the cell reference for *pr*.
- Highlight cell F2, left-click on the lower right hand corner, hold, and drag across the next two cells to right. This copies the formula for *pl/pr*, and *m/pr*.

=B2/D2					
C	D	E	F	G	H
	pR	m	pb/pr	pl/pr	m/pr
6.95	1.11	25088	1.603604		
7.32	0.67	26561			

- Label the next four columns for the logs of the data, labeling them *lnq, lnpb/pr, lnpl/pr, and lnm/pr*.
- Calculate the natural log of *q* in cell I2 by typing **=LN(A2)**, where cell A2 contains the first observation on *q*.
- Calculate the natural log of *pb/pr* in cell J2 by typing **=LN(F2)**.
- Highlight cell J2, left-click on the lower right hand corner, hold, and drag across the next two cells to right. This copies the formula for the other variables.
- Highlight the section of cells containing the log formulas (I2 to L2).
- Left-click on the lower right hand corner of the selection, hold, and drag down the column to copy the formulas down to row 31.

=LN(A2)					
G	H	I	J	K	L
r	m/pr	lnq	lnpb/pr	lnpl/pr	lnm/pr
61261	22601.8	4.403054	0.472253	1.834382	10.02578
92537	39643.28				
85542	30734.94				
73333	36210.67				
37736	25624.53				

- Choose **Tools/Data Analysis/Regression** to estimate the regression model.
- Use *lnq* as the **Y-Range**. Use *lnpb/pr, lnpl/pr,* and *lnm/pr* as the **X-Range**.
- Include labels, and check the **Labels** box.
- Place the output on a new worksheet named *reg1*.
- Click **OK**.

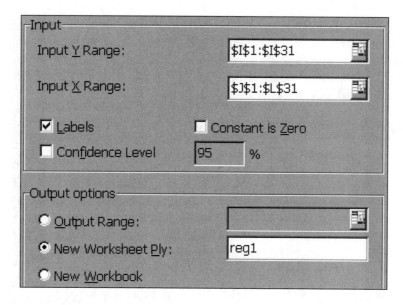

- In cell A21, type **b4*=** as a label.
- In cell B21, type **=-B18-B19-B20** to calculate $b_4^* = -b_2^*-b_3^*-b_5^*$, where cells B18, B19, and B20 contain the respective estimates.

The restricted least squares estimates are

16		Coefficients	Standard Error	t Stat	P-value
17	Intercept	-4.797797821	3.713904838	-1.291847269	0.207775849
18	lnpb/pr	-1.299386493	0.165737614	-7.840021718	2.57799E-08
19	lnpl/pr	0.186815847	0.284383243	0.656915806	0.517008173
20	lnm/pr	0.94582863	0.427046808	2.214812552	0.035742206
21	b4*=	0.166742015			

Recall that the log-log model specification provides estimates of <u>elasticities</u>, not marginal effects. Substituting these results back into our specification, we have

$$\widehat{\ln(q)} = -4.798 - 1.299\ln(p_B) + .187\ln(p_L) + .167\ln(p_R) + .946\ln(m).$$

From the results, we find that demand for beer is price elastic ($b_2 < -1$), does not seem to be affected by the price of other liquor (β_3 is not statistically significant), and might be an inferior good ($\beta_5 < 1$), although this would have to be formally tested.

Note: While some statistical packages have options to automatically estimate restricted least squares estimates, Excel does not.

8.6 Model Specification

One important consideration in building a good econometric model is the choice of explanatory variables. Leaving important variables out or including unimportant variables should be avoided. Another important choice for the econometrician is which functional form should be used in order to satisfy the assumptions of the regression model. In this section, we will develop a test, called RESET (Regression

Specification Error Test), to detect omitted variables or model misspecification.   RESET is basically an F-test where the restricted model is the "original" model and the unrestricted model is a polynomial approximation including the predicted y_t's squared and cubed as explanatory variables.   The general foundation of the test is that if the model is improved by artificially including powers of the predicted values, then the original model must not have been adequate.

8.6.1 Testing the Log-Log Model Specification

Let's use the beer demand example to illustrate RESET. We will not impose any nonsample information at this time to allow for easier discrimination among models. The restricted model is

$$ln(q) = \beta_1 + \beta_2 ln(p_B) + \beta_3 ln(p_L) + \beta_4 ln(p_R) + \beta_5 ln(m) + e.$$

The unrestricted model is

$$\ln(q) = \beta_1 + \beta_2 \ln(p_B) + \beta_3 \ln(p_L) + \beta_4 \ln(p_R) + \beta_5 \ln(m) + \gamma_1 \widehat{\ln(q)} + \gamma_2 \left[\widehat{\ln(q)}\right]^2 + e$$

and the null hypotheses are H_0: $\gamma_1 = 0$, $\gamma_2 = 0$ against the alternative that at least one γ does not equal 0. We must now create the variables needed for the regressions.

- So as not to clutter our data worksheet too much, **open** the file *table8-3.dat* once again.
- **Save As** the Excel workbook file *reset.xls*.
- Create new columns for the natural logs of all the variables, *lnq*, *ln(pb)*, *ln(pl)*, *ln(pr)*, and *ln(m)*.
- Type **=LN(A2)** in cell F2.
- Copy this formula into the four cells to the right (G2 through J2).
- Highlight cells F2 through J2.
- Copy these formulas down the column to row 31.

=LN(A2)					
E	F	G	H	I	J
	lnq	ln(pb)	ln(pl)	ln(pr)	ln(m)
25088	4.403054	0.576613	1.938742	0.10436	10.13014
26561					
25510					
27158					
27162					

- Run a regression on these data, using *lnq* as the **Y-Range**, and *ln(pb)*, *ln(pl)*, *ln(pr)*, and *ln(m)* as the **X-Range**.
- Place the output on a new worksheet called *restrict1*.
- Check the **Residuals** box. This is needed to obtain the predicted y-values.
- Click **OK**.

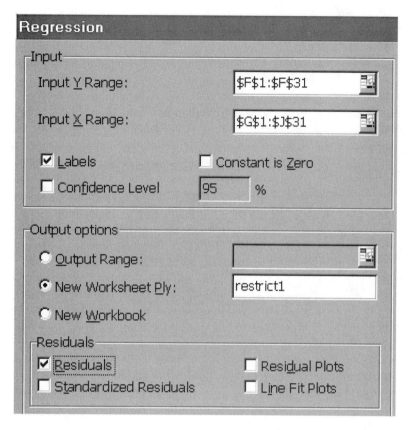

First, we will need the sum squared residuals from this regression for our SSE_R in the F-test.

- **Right-click** on cell C13 from the regression output. Choose **Copy**.

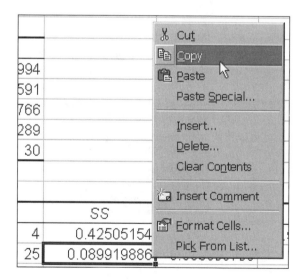

- **Open** the file *ftesttemplate.xls*.
- Place the cursor in cell B6 of the template.
- **Right click** and choose **Paste**. The value .089919886 should appear.
- Return to the *restrict1* worksheet in the *reset.xls* workbook.
- Scroll down until the residual output appears.

- Highlight cells **B27 to B57**, which contain the predicted *ln(q)*.
- Choose **Edit/Copy** from the menu bar.
- Move to the worksheet containing the original data.
- Highlight cells **K1 through K31**.
- Choose **Edit/Paste** from the menu.
- Now create two new columns, *yhat2* and *yhat3* in columns L and M.
- In cell L2, type =**K2^2**.
- In cell K2, type =**K2^3**.
- Highlight both cells L2 and K2. **Copy** the formulas down to row 31.

K	L	M
Predicted lnq	yhat2	yhat3
4.40882913	19.43777	85.69783
4.07732871		
4.14167528		
4.18815554		
4.18756721		

Recall that when you perform a regression in Excel, all of the explanatory variables must be in adjacent cells, which at this point they are not.

- Click on the K of column K to highlight it.
- Place the cursor on the edge of the highlighted area until it turns into an arrow. Left click, hold down, and drag to the right, say to column N. Release the mouse button, and now the column has been moved.

	Predicted lnq	
J	K	
)	*Predicted lnq*	yh
13014	4.40882913	1
.1872	4.07732871	1
14683	4.14167528	1

- Highlight column K once more. Choose **Edit/Delete** on the menu bar.
- Run a regression, using *lnq* as the **Y-Range**.
- Choose *ln(pb), ln(pl), ln(pr), ln(m), yhat2,* and *yhat3* as the **X-Range**.
- Place the output on a worksheet named *unrestrict*.
- Do **not** choose the Residuals option.

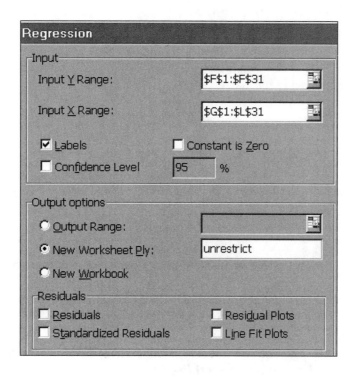

- Click **OK**.
- Copy the sum squared residuals from this regression to the cell B7 of *ftesttemplate.xls*.
- Fill in the **Data Input** values for the *F*-test. *J*=2, *T*=30, and *K*=7.

The results of the *F*-test are

	A	B
1	Hypothesis Testing Using the F-Distribution	
2	**Data Input**	
3	J	2
4	T	30
5	K	7
6	SSE-Restricted	0.089919886
7	SSE-Unrestricted	0.08720439
8	Alpha	0.05
9	**Computed Values**	
10	df-numerator	2
11	df-denominator	23
12	F	0.358103609
13	Right Critical Value	3.422130135
14	Decision	Fail to Reject Ho
15	p-value	0.702829362

We fail to reject the null hypotheses and conclude that the log-log specification is adequate.

8.6.2 Testing the Linear Model Specification

What if we had chosen a linear functional form, instead of the log-log specification? Let's test, using RESET, whether the linear model is adequate.

The restricted model is

$$q_t = \beta_1 + \beta_2 p_{Bt} + \beta_3 p_{Lt} + \beta_4 p_{Rt} + \beta_5 m_t + e_t .$$

The unrestricted model includes the squares and cubes of the predicted q_t.

$$q_t = \beta_1 + \beta_2 p_{Bt} + \beta_3 p_{Lt} + \beta_4 p_{Rt} + \beta_5 m_t + \gamma_1 \hat{q}_t^2 + \gamma_2 \hat{q}_t^3 + e_t .$$

We test the hypotheses H_0: $\gamma_1 = \gamma_2 = 0$ versus the alternative that $\gamma_1 \neq 0$, $\gamma_2 \neq 0$, or both do not equal zero.

- Return to the worksheet containing the original data in the workbook *reset.xls*
- To keep things "neat", highlight columns A through E.
- Choose **Edit/Copy** from the menu.
- Insert a new worksheet into the workbook. (Right click on a tab in lower left hand corner, **Insert/Worksheet**, etc). Name this worksheet *linear.*
- From this worksheet, Right-click and choose **Paste**.
- Run a regression using this original, untransformed data. Use *q* as the **Y-Range** and *pB, pL, pR,* and *m* as the **X-Range**.
- Place the output on a worksheet named *restrict2*.
- Choose the **Residuals** option check box.

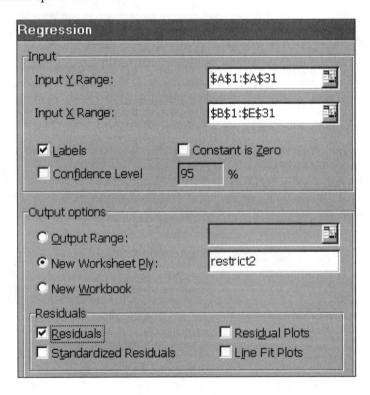

- Copy the *Predicted q* values from the residual output to column H of the *linear* worksheet.

- In columns F and G, create the variables *yhat2* and *yhat3* by squaring and cubing the values in column H. (Type **=H2^2** in cell F2 and **=H2^3** in cell G2. Copy the formulas down the column.)
- Return to the regression output on the sheet named *restrict2*.
- Copy the sum squared residual from this output to cell **B6** of *ftesttemplate.xls*.
- Return to the data on the *linear* worksheet.
- Run another regression, using *q* as the **Y-Range**, and *pB, pL, pR, m, yhat2,* and *yhat3* as the **X-Range**.
- Place the output on a sheet named *unrestrict2*.
- Do **not** choose the **Residuals** option.
- Click **OK**.

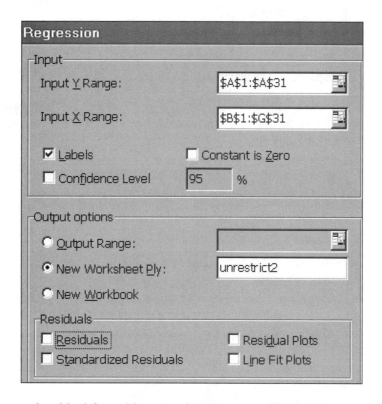

- Copy the sum squared residual from this regression output to cell **B7** of the *F*-test template.

10	ANOVA		
11		df	SS
12	Regression	6	1565.189722
13	Residual	23	225.2249448
14	Total	29	1790.414667

- Fill in the **Data Input** values; *J*=2, *T*=30, and *K*=7.

The *F*-test results are

	A	B
1	Hypothesis Testing Using the F-Distribution	
2	**Data Input**	
3	J	2
4	T	30
5	K	7
6	SSE-Restricted	318.4831049
7	SSE-Unrestricted	225.2249448
8	Alpha	0.05
9	**Computed Values**	
10	df-numerator	2
11	df-denominator	23
12	F	4.761767585
13	Right Critical Value	3.422130135
14	Decision	Reject Ho
15	p-value	0.018603559

We now reject the null hypothesis and conclude that the linear model is inadequate. Given the F-test performed in section 8.6.1, we should feel fairly confident that the log-log model specification is adequate, and the linear specification is not.

> **Note:** Such clear-cut results do not always occur. It is possible to fail to reject the null hypotheses for both a log-log model and a linear model. We should still always rely on sound economic principles when deciding on which model is "best".

8.7 Collinearity

When two or more explanatory variables are correlated, or collinear, the multiple regression model is unable to isolate individual affects on the dependent variable. Collinearity can cause high standard errors for the least squares estimators, resulting in t-tests that suggest the parameters are not significantly different from zero. Some strange results can occur, and we should be careful in interpreting our results when collinearity is present.

8.7.1 Perfect Collinearity

When there are one or more exact linear relationships between any of the explanatory variables, the least squares estimation process does not work. Many statistical packages will not even provide results, and will issue some type of error message. Excel does produce results, without any warnings or error messages.

- Open the workbook used back in chapter three called *ch3.xls*. Recall that the variables are weekly food expenditures and weekly income.
- Next to the income column, create another column called *2income+1*.
- In the first empty cell of this column, type **=2*B2+1**. This creates a variable that is a perfect linear function of weekly income.
- Copy the formula down the column.
- Run a regression, using *food expenditures* as the **Y-Range**, *income* and *2income+1* as the **X-Range**.
- No special options are needed. (In fact, you don't even need to save these results. When finished viewing the results, you can close the file without saving.)

The results are

	Coefficients	Standard Error	t Stat	P-value	Lower 95%	Upper 95%
Intercept	40.666421	0	65535	#NUM!	40.666421	40.666421
X=Income	-0.0739823	0	65535	#NUM!	-0.07398232	-0.0739823
2income+1	0.10113546	0	65535	#NUM!	0.101135462	0.1011355

While Excel did not give any warning of an error, clearly there is a problem here. Standard errors are zero, *t*-stats are huge, the *p*-values can't even be calculated, and the confidence intervals are not even intervals. If perfect collinearity exists, it will be evident from the strange regression results.

8.7.2 Identifying "Harmful" Collinearity

More commonly, we face situations where the collinearity is not perfect, but can be "harmful". When linear relationships between our explanatory variables are strong enough, high standard errors, low *t*-statistics, and unstable estimates result. We should, therefore, look to see if our results are being affected by collinearity. There are several things to look at when trying to determine the existence of this type of problem, correlation and something we call an auxiliary regression.

To explore the ways of identifying collinearity, we will use data from a production function using several different inputs. Output (Y) is a function of capital (K), labor (L), energy (E), and other intermediate materials (M). The model is

$$Y_t = \beta_1 + \beta_2 K_t + \beta_3 L_t + \beta_4 E_t + \beta_5 M_t + e_t$$

- Open the file named *manuf.dat* and immediately **Save As** *manuf.xls*.
- Run a regression, using Y_t as the **Y-Range** and K_t, L_t, E_t, and M_t as the **X-Range**.

A portion of the results is

ANOVA					
	df	SS	MS	F	Significance F
Regression	4	2.938798893	0.734699723	107.2566345	3.24356E-13
Residual	20	0.136998467	0.006849923		
Total	24	3.07579736			
	Coefficients	Standard Error	t Stat	P-value	Lower 95%
Intercept	-0.051802423	0.235826984	-0.219662832	0.828360201	-0.543728662
K	0.098431434	0.230195828	0.427598688	0.673512038	-0.381748425
L	0.427889549	0.456477786	0.937372118	0.359749716	-0.524305985
E	-0.09604997	0.339893017	-0.28258883	0.780395926	-0.805054049
M	0.662084894	0.310918273	2.129449929	0.045828801	0.013521043

According to the *Significance F*, the model is statistically significant. At least one of the model's parameters is not equal to zero. However, when we test each parameter individually, using *t*-tests, we find that *M* is significant at the 5% level but not at the 1% level. No other inputs seem to be important in determining output. This goes against what standard economic theory would say. This is a "clue" that collinearity may be causing problems; the model is significant, but many important explanatory variables are not.   Remember, collinearity can cause low *t*-stats.   These regression results seem to be consistent with this problem.

Since collinearity exists when two or more independent variables are linearly related, a simple way the check the strength of possible linearity is to look at the correlation matrix.   Correlation measures the direction and strength of a linear relationship between two variables.

- Return to the worksheet containing the original data.
- With the cursor in an empty cell, choose **Tools/Data Analysis/Correlation**.

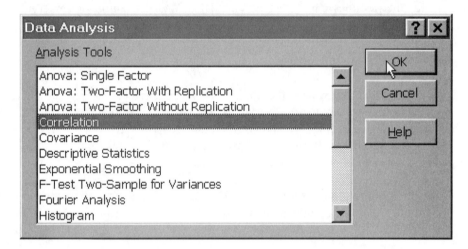

- In the **Input Range**, include the four explanatory variables, *K, L, E,* and *M* and their labels.
- Check the **Labels in First Row** box.
- Place the output on a new worksheet named *corr*.
- Click **OK**.

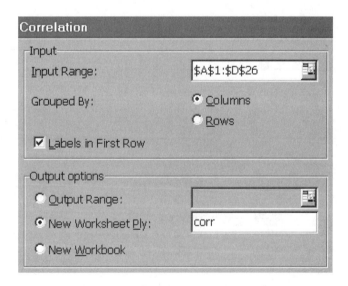

The correlation matrix is

	A	B	C	D	E
1		K	L	E	M
2	K	1			
3	L	0.946011	1		
4	E	0.986941	0.966794	1	
5	M	0.964521	0.98351	0.97981	1

These results show the high degree of linearity between all of the variables. However, correlation only measures the pair-wise linearity between variables. A more complex linear relationship between several variables at a time is not detected by correlation. Here, however, we have pretty good evidence that collinearity exists.

To detect more complex linear relationships, we will use the coefficient of determination, R^2, introduced in chapter six. Recall that R^2 is interpreted as the percent of the total variation in the dependent variable that is explained by the model, or the explanatory variables. This interpretation is very helpful now.

An auxiliary regression is a multiple regression, but one of the original explanatory variables is used as the dependent variable. We are not concerned with any of the regression output except the R^2, because it measures how much of the variation in that one explanatory variable is explained, or being determined by, the other explanatory variables. This is, then, a measure of collinearity. To pick which variable to use as the dependent variable in this auxiliary regression, you would choose the explanatory variable that seems to be related to other variables the most, from the correlation matrix. In our example, no one variable seems to stand out, so we will simply choose one, let's say K.

- Return to the worksheet containing the original data.
- Run a regression, using K as the **Y-Range**, and L, E, and M as the **X-Range**.
- Place the output on a worksheet called *aux*.

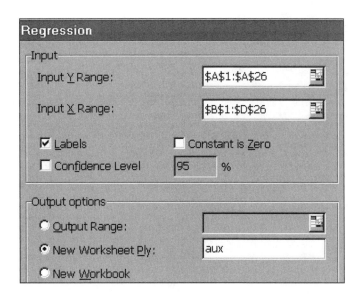

The only output we are interested in is the R^2 from this auxiliary regression.

	A	B
1	SUMMARY OUTPUT	
2		
3	*Regression Statistics*	
4	Multiple R	0.987562
5	R Square	0.975279
6	Adjusted R Square	0.971747
7	Standard Error	0.078458
8	Observations	25

97.5% of the variation in capital is explained by the other explanatory variables. That means only 2.5% of the variation in capital is independent of the other variables! Put this together with the values of the correlation matrix, and it seems pretty evident that we have a collinearity problem.

Usually, increasing our sample size increases the precision of the least squares estimators. In this case, however, simply adding more observations just adds more collinear data. The solution is to obtain new, better data. But this is often impossible. One other solution may be to impose nonsample information on the model, as we did earlier in this chapter. Beware, however, for if the restrictions we place on the model are not exactly true, our restricted estimators are biased.

Chapter 9 Dummy (Binary) Variables

Thus far, we have assumed that the parameters of our regression model are the same for each observation. There are situations, however, where this assumption may not hold and we want to be able to allow the regression parameters to take on different values for different observations. Dummy variables, or binary variables, are used to allow for parameter variation based on some qualitative characteristic. In this chapter, we will use dummy variables to allow the intercept to differ, and to allow the slope parameters to differ across some of the observations.

9.1 The University Effect on House Prices

An important issue in the real estate industry is how to accurately predict the price of a house, based on several of its characteristics, including the ever-important "location, location, location". Economists commonly use a "hedonic" model of pricing based on several characteristics such as size, location, number of bedrooms, age, etc. Using a dummy variable, D_t, which is equal to 1 if the house is in a desirable neighborhood and is equal to 0 if the house is not in a desirable neighborhood captures the qualitative factor, location. Including this variable in the regression model will allow the intercept to be different for houses in desirable areas compared to the intercept for houses not in desirable areas.

We also allow for different slopes for houses in different areas by including an interaction variable, the product of the dummy variable and one of the continuous explanatory variables. One variable used to explain the price of houses is its size in square feet ($SQFT_t$). We might believe that an extra square foot of living space of a house in a good neighborhood affects the price differently than a house not in a good neighborhood. To allow for this in our model, we create the interaction variable, $SQFT_t \times D_t$, and include it as an explanatory variable in our price model. The full model we will estimate is

$$PRICE_t = \beta_1 + \delta_1 UTOWN_t + \beta_2 SQFT_t + \gamma(SQFT_t \times UTOWN_t) + \beta_3 AGE_t + \delta_2 POOL_t + \delta_3 FPLACE_t + e_t$$

where $PRICE =$ the price of the house, in dollars
$UTOWN = 1$ for houses near the university (desirable), 0 otherwise
$SQFT =$ number of square feet of living area
$AGE =$ age of house in years
$POOL = 1$ if house has a pool, 0 otherwise
$FPLACE = 1$ if house has a fireplace, 0 otherwise.

Note that this model contains two continuous explanatory variables ($SQFT$ and AGE), and three dummy variables, capturing the qualitative characteristics of location, presence of a pool, and a fireplace. Let's now estimate this model.

- Open the data file named *table9-1.dat*. **Save As** an Excel workbook called *houseprice.xls*.

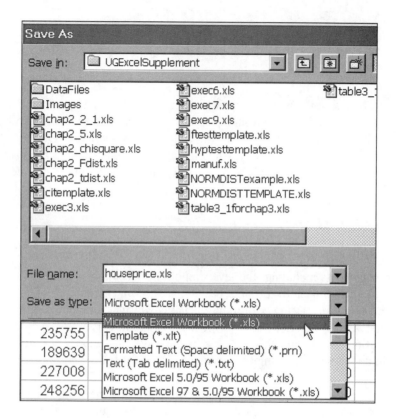

- Label column G *sqftXUtown*.
- In cell G2 create the interaction variable by typing **=B2*D2**.
- Copy this formula down the column to row 1001.

=B2*D2					
C	D	E	F	G	
	Utown	Pool	Fplace	sqftXUtown	
6	0	0	1	0	
5	0	0	1		
6	0	0	0		
1	0	0	0		
0	0	0	1		

Zeros appear in column G down to row 482. Then different values appear after that. This is because the variable *UTOWN* is equal to zero through row 482, then one after that.

- Run a regression (**Tools/Data Analysis/Regression**) using column A as the **Y-Range** and columns B through G as the **X-Range**.
- Include labels and check the **Labels** box.
- Save to a new worksheet called *reg1*.

The parameter estimates and corresponding *t*-stats and *p*-values are

16		Coefficients	Standard Error	t Stat	P-value
17	Intercept	24499.98487	6191.72142	3.956893925	8.13332E-05
18	sqft	76.12176558	2.451764659	31.04774567	1.8675E-148
19	age	-190.086422	51.20460724	-3.712291379	0.000216812
20	Utown	27452.95224	8422.582357	3.259445984	0.001154211
21	Pool	4377.16329	1196.691644	3.657720276	0.000267837
22	Fplace	1649.175634	971.9568188	1.69675813	0.090055789
23	sqftXUtown	12.99404898	3.320477528	3.913307311	9.72453E-05

From these results, we conclude that all of the parameters are significant, using a one-tailed 5% level test. (Remember that Excel reports *p*-values for a two-tailed test). The interpretations of the coefficients on *AGE*, *POOL*, and *FPLACE* are as usual. But to conclude that the δ_1 is statistically different from zero means that there IS a shift in the intercept for houses near the university. Similarly, concluding that γ is different from zero means that the marginal effect of the size of the house IS different for houses near the university. But Excel doesn't know that we have allowed the intercept and the coefficient on *SQFT* to differ across observations. It is our responsibility to correctly determine the intercept and slope estimates. Looking at the original model that we estimated

$$PRICE_t = \beta_1 + \delta_1 UTOWN_t + \beta_2 SQFT_t + \gamma(SQFT_t \times UTOWN_t) + \beta_3 AGE_t + \delta_2 POOL_t + \delta_3 FPLACE_t + e_t$$

we see that the intercept is $\beta_1 + \delta_1$ when *UTOWN* is equal to one, and is simply β_1 when *UTOWN* is zero. Similarly, the coefficient on *SQFT* when *UTOWN* is one is equal to $\beta_2 + \gamma$, and is equal to β_2 when *UTOWN* is zero. We can calculate the estimates for these parameters on the Excel regression output worksheet.

- In cell A24, type the label *newintercept*. In cell A25, type the label *newbeta2.*

- In cell B24, type **=B17+B20** to calculate the intercept when *UTOWN* is equal to one.
- In cell B25, type **=B18+B23** to calculate the coefficient estimate for *SQFT* when *UTOWN* is equal to one.

16		Coefficients
17	Intercept	24499.9848705457
18	sqft	76.1217655809397
19	age	-190.086422001159
20	Utown	27452.9522392834
21	Pool	4377.16329042294
22	Fplace	1649.17563442081
23	sqftXUtown	12.9940489843786
24	newintercept	=B17+B20
25	newbeta2	=B18+B23

We now report two estimated regression functions. For houses near the university

$$\hat{PRICE} = 51952.94 + 89.12SQFT - 190.09AGE + 4377.16POOL + 1649.17FPLACE$$

For houses not close to the university

$$\hat{PRICE} = 24499.98 + 76.12SQFT - 190.09AGE + 4377.16POOL + 1649.17FPLACE$$

From these results, there appears to be a "location premium" worth \$27,453 on houses close to the university, and a square foot of living area in a house near the university is worth \$12.99 more than a square foot of living area in a house not near the university.

9.2   Testing the Equivalence of Two Regressions Using Dummy Variables

In the last section, we find that the intercept and one of the "slopes" differ when using the *t*-tests for individual significance. Now, we might assume that location affects both the intercept and the slope, jointly. A simplified model is

$$P_t = \beta_1 + \delta D_t + \beta_2 S_t + \gamma(S_t D_t) + e_t$$

We could perform a joint test, H_0: $\delta=0$, $\gamma=0$ and if we fail to reject this hypothesis, we would conclude that the data from the two neighborhoods can be "pooled" since there is no evidence that the intercept or the slope are different. If we reject the null, we should not ignore location effects. We should not pool the data, but instead, run two separate regressions. Testing the equivalence of two regressions in this way is called a Chow test and is based on an F-test.

9.2.1 A Chow Test

Recall that an F-test is based on comparing the sum of the squared errors from a restricted and an unrestricted model. This is still true, where now the restricted model assumes no structural change (no difference in the intercept or slopes) across the regressions.

The model we will use to perform a Chow test is based on the investment strategies of two similar firms, General Electric and Westinghouse. Investment (INV) is a function of the value of the firm (proxied by the value of the firm's stock, V), and the firm's stock of capital (K). The restricted model is

$$INV_t = \beta_1 + \beta_2 V_t + \beta_3 K_t + e_t$$

The unrestricted model allows the intercept and slope coefficients to differ for the two firms. To model these possibilities, we create a dummy variable, D_t, which takes on a value of one for the 20 Westinghouse observations, and zero for the General Electric observations. Including the intercept dummy variable and a complete set of interaction variables, the unrestricted model is

$$INV_t = \beta_1 + \delta_1 Dt + \beta_2 V_t + \delta_2 (D_t V_t) + \beta_3 K_t + \delta_3 (D_t K_t) + e_t$$

Testing the equivalence of these two models is done by testing H_0: $\delta_1=0$, $\delta_2=0$, $\delta_3=0$ against the alternative that at least one δ_k does not equal zero. We will use the F-test template created in chapter 8.

- Open the file created in chapter 8 named *ftesttemplate.xls*.
- Open the data file *table9-3.dat* and **Save As** an Excel workbook called *GEWH_inv.xls*.
- You will need to move some data around to have the values listed in contiguous columns. **Highlight D1 through D21.**
- Place the cursor on the edge of the highlighted area and **left click**. **Hold down** and **drag** the selection to A22:A42. **Release** the left mouse button.
- Click on the number 22 of row 22.
- Choose **Edit**, **Delete**. You must now remember that Westinghouse observations start with row 22.

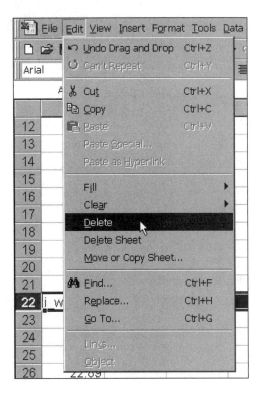

- **Move** the Westinghouse stock value and capital variables in a similar fashion to columns B and C.
- **Delete** the rows containing the labels for Westinghouse.

- **Label** column D the dummy variable, *D*. (Just a coincidence!)
- Since the first 20 observations are for GE, **type a 0** in cell D2.
- **Copy** the value down the column through D21.
- **Type a 1** in cell D22. Copy this down the remainder of the column.

21	189.6	2759.9	888.9	0
22	12.93	191.5	1.8	1
23	25.9	516	0.8	
24	35.05	729	7.4	
25	22.89	560.4	18.1	
26	18.84	519.9	23.5	

- Label column E *DV* and column F *DK*.
- In cell E2 type **=B2*D2.**
- In cell F2 type **=C2*D2**.
- **Highlight** both cells E2 and F2.
- **Copy** the formulas down the column to row 41. Notice the first 20 observations are zero, then values equal to *V* and *K* after that.

=B2*D2				
C	D	E	F	
e	D	DV	DK	
97.8	0	0	0	
104.4	0			
118	0			
156.2	0			
172.6	0			
186.6	0			
220.9	0			

Now we are ready to run two regressions, one using only *V* and *K* as explanatory variables, the other using *V* and *K* and the dummy variable and interactions variables.

- Choose **Tools/Data Analysis/Regression.**
- Use the data in column A for the **Y-Range**.
- Use the data in columns B and C for the **X-Range**.
- Place the results on a worksheet named *restricted.*

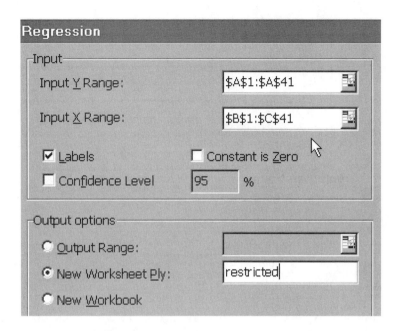

- Now run another regression, but include columns B through F in the **X-Range**.
- Place the results on a worksheet named *unrestricted.*

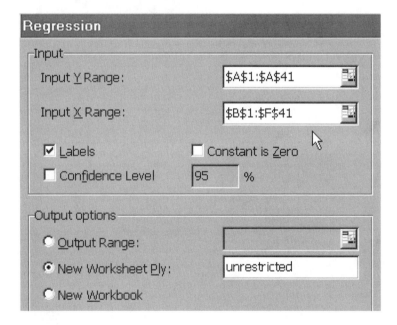

- **Copy** the SS Residual from the *restricted* worksheet to cell B6 of *ftesttemplate.xls.*
- **Copy** the SS Residual from the *unrestricted* worksheet to cell B7 of *ftesttemplate.xls.*
- Fill in the Data Input, using values from the unrestricted model. *J*=3, *T*=40, and *K*=6.

The results of this Chow test are

	A	B
1	Hypothesis Testing Using the F-Distribution	
2	**Data Input**	
3	J	3
4	T	40
5	K	6
6	SSE-Restricted	16563.00338
7	SSE-Unrestricted	14989.8217
8	Alpha	0.05
9	**Computed Values**	
10	df-numerator	3
11	df-denominator	34
12	F	1.189433255
13	Right Critical Value	2.882600825
14	Decision	Fail to Reject Ho
15	p-value	0.328351499

We fail to the reject the null hypotheses and conclude that there is no structural difference in the two regressions. Since it appears there is no difference in the intercept or any of the slopes, we can pool the data and assume the results from the restricted model above are "correct".

Chapter 10 Nonlinear Models

The least squares estimation procedure we have been using is based on the assumption that the model is linear in the parameters, though not necessarily linear in the variables. We saw in chapter 8 the total revenue model with diminishing marginal returns to advertising expenditures. To allow for this effect, we included the square of advertising expenditures as another explanatory variable. In chapter 9, we used an interaction variable (a dummy variable multiplied to a continuous variable) to allow the marginal effects of the size of a house to differ across some of the observations. By transforming the variables to capture these different effects, we still did not violate the assumptions of the linear regression model.

In this chapter, we will look at more models where the response to a change in the explanatory variable depends on the value of that variable or the value of another variable. We use interaction variables that are the product of an explanatory variable and itself, and interaction variables that are the product of two different explanatory variables. These models are still linear in the parameters, not a violation of our assumptions.

Models that have parameters that are nonlinear require *nonlinear least squares estimation*, as described in Chapter 10.2 of *UE/2*. As we have seen, Excel is a powerful spreadsheet. It is not designed to be a complete econometric software package, and consequently it does not have the capabilities to estimate models that are nonlinear in the parameters. If you encounter such a problem, use econometric software such as EViews, Shazam, or SAS.

10.1 Polynomial Terms in a Regression Model

In economics, we deal often with cost functions; total cost, average cost, and marginal cost. These curves are related to each other, and are also the mirror images of the product curves. Total cost curves are typically "cubic" shapes, and the average and marginal cost curves are quadratic in shape. By using the square and cubes of total output, we can easily estimate these cost functions using Excel. A simple transformation of the data is all that is needed.

The average cost function is

$$AC = \beta_1 + \beta_2 Q + \beta_3 Q^2 + e$$

The slope of this function is

$$\frac{dE(AC)}{dQ} = \beta_2 + 2\beta_3 Q$$

The total cost function is

$$TC = \alpha_1 + \alpha_2 Q + \alpha_3 Q^2 + \alpha_4 Q^3 + e$$

and the slope (and marginal cost!) is

$$\frac{dE(TC)}{dQ} = \alpha_2 + 2\alpha_3 Q + 3\alpha_4 Q^2$$

- Open the data file named *cloth.dat* and **Save As** an Excel worksheet named *costs.xls*. The file contains total cost (*C1* and *C2*) and total output (*Q1* and *Q2*) for two firms. Since we only need data on one firm,
- Delete columns C and D by highlighting the columns, then choose **Edit/Delete**.

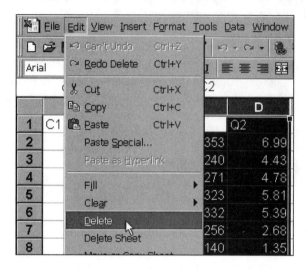

- Type the label **Q2** in cell C1. Type the label **Q3** in cell D1.
- In cells C2 and D2, type the formulas **=B2^2** and **=B2^3** respectively.
- **Copy** these formulas down the column.

- Run a regression to estimate the average cost function. Use *C1* as the **Y-Range** and *Q1* and *Q2* as the **X-Range**.
- Include labels.
- Place the output on a worksheet named *avgcost*.

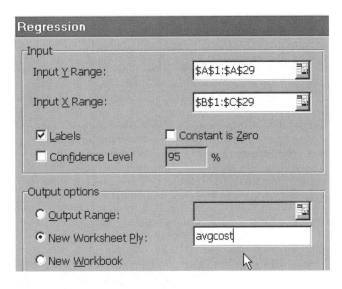

The results of this regression are

16		Coefficients	Standard Error	t Stat	P-value
17	Intercept	208.635038	23.27801486	8.962750442	2.7854E-09
18	Q1	-14.65459261	9.766522385	-1.5004924	0.146011635
19	Q2	6.119402401	0.868717752	7.044177912	2.20279E-07

b_2 is negative and b_3 is positive, as expected. This produces the convex shape of a typical average cost curve. Note, however, that β_2 is only significant at the 10% level.

- Run another regression to estimate the total cost function. Use *C1* as the **Y-Range** and *Q1, Q2* and *Q3* as the **X-Range**.
- Include labels.
- Place the output on a worksheet named *totcost*.

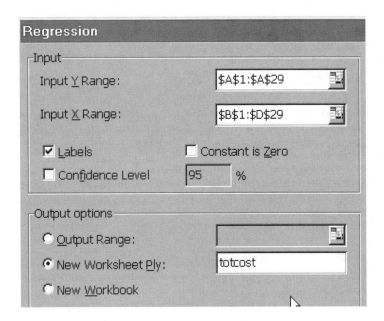

The results of this regression are

16		Coefficients	Standard Error	t Stat	P-value
17	Intercept	72.77426169	35.7335275	2.036582078	0.052869022
18	Q1	83.65859433	23.65464536	3.536666607	0.001682453
19	Q2	-13.79592578	4.596830564	-3.001182138	0.00618833
20	Q3	1.191122379	0.272075109	4.377917488	0.000202044

For a typical U-shaped marginal cost curve (the "slope"of the total cost function), $\alpha_2 > 0$, $\alpha_3 < 0$, and $\alpha_4 > 0$. Our estimates are consistent with these expectations. All of the model parameters are statistically significant.

Using polynomial terms in our regression model allows us to estimate many types of nonlinear relationships between variables. Transforming the data the way we did has done nothing to violate the assumptions of the linear regression model. However, as always, care must be taken in interpreting the results!

10.2   Interactions Between Two Continuous Variables

When we include the product of two continuous explanatory variables in a model, we alter the relationship between each of them and the dependent variable. Reporting and interpreting the results are not as straight forward as in simpler models, but you, the econometrician, will have no trouble dealing with this special case.

The model we use here is based on a "life-cycle" model of the effects of age and income on a person's expenditures on pizza. We believe that as a person ages, the marginal effect of income will probably change (the marginal propensity to spend on pizza probably falls). Since we assume that the effect of income depends on age, we include an interaction variable that is the product of these two variables. The model we will estimate is

$$PIZZA = \beta_1 + \beta_2 AGE + \beta_3 Y + \beta_4(AGE \times Y) + e$$

where $PIZZA$ = individuals' annual expenditure on pizza, in dollars
AGE = the age of the individual in years
Y = the annual income of the individual, in dollars

To find the marginal effects of age and income, we take the first derivative of the function above, with respect to the variable of interest. We find that the marginal effect of age on pizza expenditures is $\beta_2 + \beta_4 Y$ and the effect of income is $\beta_3 + \beta_4 AGE$. These will be estimated and calculated using Excel.

- Open the file named *table10-1.dat* and immediately **Save As** an Excel workbook named *pizza.xls*.
- Insert a row at the top of the data file so you can label the data. Highlight row 1 and choose **Insert/Rows** from the menu.

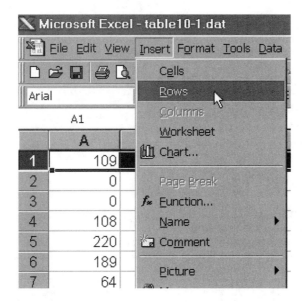

- Label the data appropriately. Column A is *Pizza*, column B is *Y* (income), and column C is *Age*.
- Label column D *Age*Y*.
- In cell D2, type **=B2*C2** to create the interaction variable.
- Copy the formula down the column.
- Run a regression, using *Pizza* as the **Y-Range** and *Y, Age,* and *Age*Y* as the **X-Range**.
- Include labels and place the output on a worksheet named *reg1*.

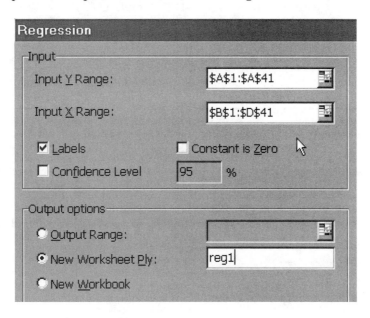

The results of this estimation are

16		Coefficients	Standard Error	t Stat	P-value
17	Intercept	161.465432	120.6634096	1.338147434	0.189239689
18	Y	0.009073877	0.003669598	2.472716864	0.01826628
19	Age	-2.977423365	3.352100814	-0.88822608	0.380315589
20	Age*Y	-0.000160211	8.67343E-05	-1.847147792	0.072957528

Not shown are the Summary Output and ANOVA, however the model is statistically significant. Now we will create a template for calculating the estimated marginal effects, using estimates of the formulas presented above.

- In cell A21, type the label *age level =*.
- In cell A22, type the label *income level =*.
- In cell A23, type the label *age effect =*.
- In cell A24, type the label *income effect =*.
- In cell B23, type **=B19+(B20*B22)**.
- In cell B24, type **=B18+(B20*B21)**.

This template can now be used to calculate the marginal effects, given any level of age and/or income. Simply provide the input for cells B21 and B22.

16		*Coefficients*
17	Intercept	161.465432008407
18	Y	0.00907387659114657
19	Age	-2.97742336532075
20	Age*Y	-0.000160211156533084
21	age level=	
22	income level =	
23	age effect =	=B19+(B20*B22)
24	income effect =	=B18+(B20*B21)

- In cell A22, type the value 25,000 and observe the result in cell B23.
- Next, change the value in cell A22 to 90,000 and observe the results.

21	age level=	
22	income level =	25000
23	age effect =	-6.982702279
24	income effect =	#VALUE!

21	age level=	
22	income level =	90000
23	age effect =	-17.39642745
24	income effect =	#VALUE!

As the results show, as a person ages one year, they decrease their expenditures on pizza more at an income of $90,000 versus $25,000. ($17.40 less versus $6.98 less). The results do suggest that, overall, people decrease their expenditures on pizza as they grow older.

- In cell B21, type a value of 25 and observe the results.
- Next, change the value in cell B21 to 50 and observe the results.

21	age level=	25
22	income level =	
23	age effect =	#VALUE!
24	income effect =	0.005068598

21	age level=	50
22	income level =	
23	age effect =	#VALUE!
24	income effect =	0.001063319

When a person 25 years old has an increase of $1000 in their income, they buy $5.00 more pizza, while a person who is 50 only buys $1.00 more when their income increases by $1000.

Chapter 11 Heteroskedasticity

One of the assumptions of the linear regression model is that the variance of the error term (and of the dependent variable) is constant across all of the observations. If this assumption is not met, Excel will still produce regression estimates, but the standard errors of the least squares estimators are computed incorrectly. We use the standard errors to make inferences about our parameters, and our conclusions could also be incorrect.

In this chapter, we will look at the nature of heteroskedasticity ("unequal dispersion") and provide several methods for detecting it, including plotting the estimated errors and performing a formal test, called a Goldfeld-Quandt test. In addition, we will look at specific forms of heteroskedasticity and use model transformation to estimate the parameters, using *generalized least squares* estimation.

11.1 The Nature of Heteroskedasticity

In chapter 3, we introduced a model of food expenditures as a function of income. At each income level, a household chooses its level of food expenditures. It seems reasonable that households with higher incomes have more choices, anywhere from "simple" food (Spam?) to extravagant food (lobster and filet mignon?). This suggests that the variances for low-income households and high-income households are probably not equal. The consequences of estimating the parameters as we did back in chapter three, if heteroskedasticity is present, are that the standard errors that Excel reports are wrong. Therefore, the t-statistics, p-values, and confidence intervals are also wrong. Let's return to that model and our Excel results to reconsider our assumptions about the variance of the model.

- Open the file named *ch3.xls.*
- If you did not do so in chapter 3, run a regression, using food expenditures as the **Y-Range** and income as the **X-Range**. Choose **Line Fit Plots** under the Residuals option to produce a chart of the estimated regression line.

After formatting, the graph should look like

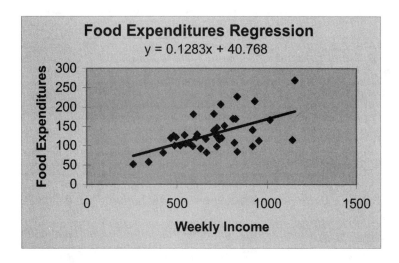

As income increases, it appears that the data points are scattered further and further from the estimated regression line. The residuals are getting larger as income increases. The parameter that determines how much the dependent variable is scattered around the mean (the regression line) is σ^2, the variance of the model, and so far, we've been assuming this is constant across all observations. The graph above, however, suggests that it is not constant, but is greater for larger income households; that is, we have heteroskedasticity.

11.2 White's Approximate Estimator for the Variance of the LS Estimator

Since, with heteroskedasticity, our reported standard errors are incorrect, we need a method for determining the correct standard errors for our least squares estimators. We can then recalculate our t-stats and confidence intervals. White's approximation of the estimator for the variance of b_2 is

$$\text{v\^ar}(b_2) = \frac{\sum \left[(x_t - \bar{x})^2 \, \hat{e}_t^2 \right]}{\left[\sum (x_t - \bar{x})^2 \right]^2}$$

The square root of this is the estimated standard error for b_2. Some statistical packages will calculate White's standard errors automatically. Excel does not, but we can use the standard Excel functions to calculate it "by hand".

- Return to the data contained in *ch3.xls*.
- Run another regression, choosing the **Residuals** option.
- From the regression output, **Copy** the residuals in cells C22 through C62 to the worksheet containing the original data. **Paste** these residuals in column C (including label).
- Label column D *ehat2* and square the values in column C here. (Type **=C^2** in cell D2 and copy the formula down the column.)
- Label column E *xbar*. In cell E2 type **=AVERAGE(A2:A41)** where column A contains food expenditures. Alternatively, you can use the Paste Function *fx* to obtain this value.
- Label column F *(x-xbar)2*. In cell F2 type **=(A2-$E$2)^2**. Recall that the dollar sign anchors the cell containing *xbar*.
- Label column G *numterm* (for "numerator term"). In cell G2 type **=F2*D2**.
- Highlight cells F2 and G2, and copy these formulas down the columns.

=(A2-$E$2)^2					
C	D	E	F	G	
esiduals	ehat2	x-bar	(x-xbar)2	numterm	
21.654502	468.9175	698	193336.1	90658668.6	
26.463375	700.3102				
13.500212	182.2557				
9.1575225	367.0107				

- In cell F42, type **=SUM(F2:F41)** to sum the column (or use the Paste Function).
- In cell G42, type **=SUM(G2:G41)**.
- Finally, label an empty cell, say B44, *White's var(b2)*.
- Label cell B45 *White's se(b2)*.
- In cell C44, type **=G42/(F42^2)**.
- In cell C45, type **=SQRT(C44)**.

The results are

40	115.43	-71.753337	5148.541		196514.9	1011765037
41	269.03	80.1404248	6422.488		208483.6	1338983096
42					1532463	3421453919
43						
44	White's var(b2)	0.0014569				
45	White's se(b2)	0.0381694				

Excel's regression output reports the standard error for b_2 as 0.030539, which is incorrect due to the heteroskedasticity. White's standard error is higher, which makes the corrected t-stat smaller and the confidence intervals wider. You should recalculate and report the *corrected* t-stat and confidence interval, do not report those produced in the regression output.

11.3 Proportional Heteroskedasticity

We saw in the graph of the regression that the estimated error terms seem to get larger as income increases. We can model this type of heteroskedasticity and actually transform our original model to one that is homoskedastic, given our assumptions about the form of the heteroskedasticity is correct.

We assume the variance of the model is proportional to income and can be modeled as $var(e_t) = \sigma_t^2 x_t$. It can be shown that, if we transform our original data by dividing all observations by the square root of x_t, the new, transformed model is homoskedastic and we can estimate the new model using least squares. This procedure is called *generalized least squares estimation* and produces standard errors (and therefore t-stats and confidence intervals) that are correct.

- Return to the worksheet containing the original data on food expenditures and income.
- To keep things neat, copy just the two original variables to a new workbook named *proporhetero.xls*.
- Label column C *sqrt(x)*.
- Label columns D, E and F, *int**, *x** and *y** respectively.
- In cell C2, type **=SQRT(A2)**, where cell A2 contains the first observation on income.
- In cell D2, type **=1/C2**. This creates a new intercept term, not equal to one anymore.
- In cell E2, type **=A2/C2**.
- In cell F2, type **=B2/C2**.
- Highlight cells C2 through F2. Copy the formulas down the column.
- Run a regression, using *y** as the **Y-Range** and *int** and *x** as the **X-Range**.
- Include labels and check the **Labels** box.
- Check the **Constant is Zero** box since we now have our new, transformed intercept term.
- Place the output on the worksheet named *gls*.
- Click **OK**.

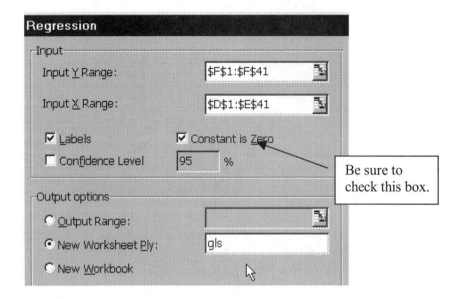

The regression results are

	Coefficients	Standard Error	t Stat	P-value	Lower 95%	Upper 95%
Intercept	0	#N/A	#N/A	#N/A	#N/A	#N/A
int*	31.92438401	17.98608167	1.7749494	0.083917306	-4.486536016	68.33530405
x*	0.140957903	0.02699529	5.221574	6.63229E-06	0.086308794	0.195607011

The estimates, b_1 and b_2, differ somewhat from those from our original regression. However, the interpretations are the same. Transforming the data in the manner we did changed a heteroskedastic model to a homoskedastic model; it did not change the meanings of our estimates. When income increases by $100, food expenditures increase by $14.10.

The standard errors reported here are lower than those we calculated using White's approximation. This is to be expected because the generalized least squares procedure is better than ("regular") least squares. The smaller standard errors produce higher t-stats and narrower (more precise) confidence intervals.

11.4 Detecting Heteroskedasticity

The particular form of heteroskedasticity in the food expenditures model was fairly easy to detect. This is not always the case. In this section, we show two ways to investigate the existence of hetero, plotting the residuals and performing the Goldfeld-Quandt test.

11.4.1 Plotting the Residuals

If our model is homoskedastic, when we plot the residuals, there should be no systematic pattern evident. If the model is heteroskedastic, we may be able to detect a particular pattern in the residuals and perhaps even discover the form of the heteroskedasticity.

- Return to the original data on food expenditures and income.
- Run a regression, using food expenditures as the **Y-Range** and income as the **X-Range**.
- Under the Residuals options, choose **Residual Plots**. This will produce a graph of the residuals, plotted against income.

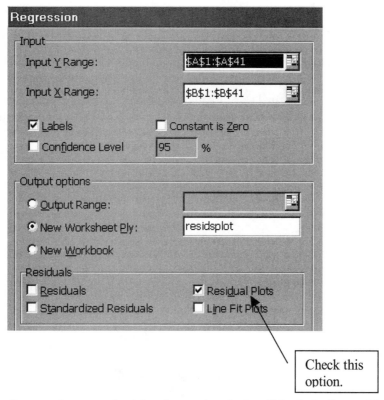

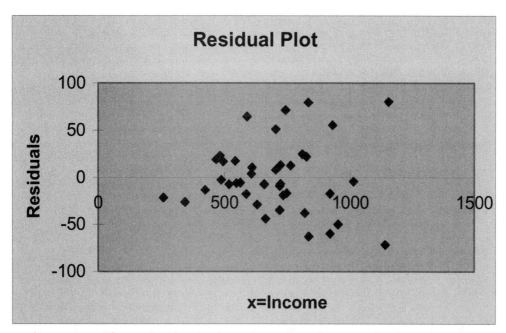

The graph will need to be formatted, as usual. After formatting, it should look similar to this.

The data points seem to "fan out" as income increases, suggesting a systematic pattern in the residuals.

Note: This method of obtaining a graph of the residuals only works with the simple regression model. When you are dealing with a multivariate model, you must obtain graphs differently. When you run the regression, choose the Residuals option. Then Copy and Paste the predicted *y*'s and the residuals into columns on the worksheet containing the original data. Use the Chart Wizard (or choose Insert/Chart from the menu) to plot the residuals against each explanatory variable, or against the predicted y's.

11.4.2 The Goldfeld-Quandt Test

The Goldfeld-Quandt test is a formal test of equal variances, a type of F-test. The basic steps are to order the data based on variance, split the data approximately in half, compute the estimated variances, calculate the test statistic $GQ = \hat{\sigma}_1^2 / \hat{\sigma}_2^2$, and compare to an F-critical value, based on T_1-K numerator and T_2-K denominator degrees of freedom. If heteroskedasticity is present, the GQ test statistic should be large, and we would reject a null hypothesis of equal variances. Let's test for hetero in our food expenditures model.   Formally, we test the null hypothesis $H_0: \sigma_t^2 = \sigma^2$ against the alternative $H_1: \sigma_t^2 = \sigma^2 x_t$.

- Copy the original data on food expenditures and income to a new workbook (for housekeeping reasons!).
- Since we suspect that the variance is "connected" to income, sort the data on income. Highlight both columns of the data, including labels.
- Choose **Data/Sort** from the menu bar.
- Click on the down-arrow in the **Sort By** box. Choose x.

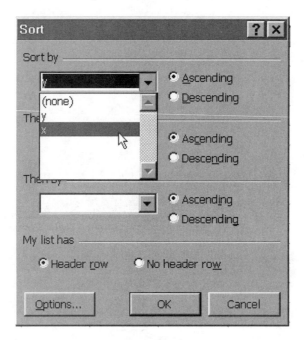

- Check the **Ascending** option.
- Check the **Header Row** option, since we included the labels.
- Click **OK**.

Looking at the column containing x (income), the numbers should be increasing as you look down the column.

	A	B
1	y	x
2	52.25	258.3
3	58.32	343.1
4	81.79	425
5	119.9	467.5
6	125.8	482.9
7	100.46	487.7
8	121.51	496.5
9	100.08	519.4
10	127.75	543.3
11	104.94	548.7
12	107.48	564.6
13	98.48	588.3

Be sure these are in ascending order.

Now we must run two regressions, using the first half of the data in the first one, and the second half of the data in the second regression. The only output we're interested in from these regressions is the estimated variance of the model.

- Run a regression on the data, using cells A2 through A21 for the **Y-Range** and cells B2 through B21 for the **X-Range**.
- Do **NOT** include labels.
- Place the output on a worksheet named *reg1*. No other options are needed.

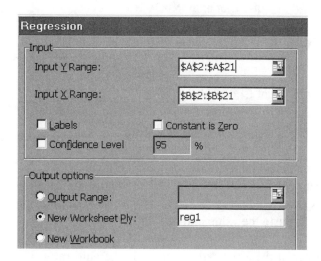

- Repeat the procedures above, but now include cells A22 through A41 as the **Y-Range** and cells B22 through B1 as the **X-Range**.
- Save output to a worksheet named *reg2*.

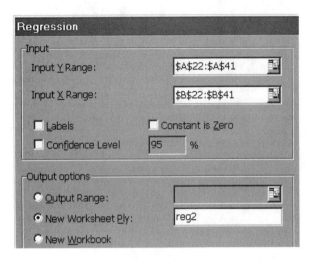

- Open a new workbook and name it *GQtest.xls*.
- Create the following template to use for any Goldfeld-Quandt test.

	A	B
1	Goldfeld-Quandt Test for Equal Variances	
2	**Data Input**	
3	T1	
4	T2	
5	K	
6	SigmaHatSquared1	
7	SigmaHatSquared2	
8	Alpha	0.05
9	**Computed Values**	
10	df-numerator	=B3-B5
11	df-denominator	=B4-B5
12	GQ	=B6/B7
13	One-Tailed Test: Right Critical Value	=FINV(B8,B10,B11)
14	Decision	=IF(B12>B13,"Reject Ho","Fail to Reject Ho")
15	p-value	=FDIST(B12,B10,B11)
16	Two-Tailed Test: Right Critical Value	=FINV(0.5*B8,B10,B11)
17	Decision	=IF(B12>B16,"Reject Ho","Fail to Reject Ho")
18	p-value	=0.5*B15

- Return to the workbook containing the two regressions you just ran.
- From the *reg1* worksheet, highlight cell D13 (the MS residual from the ANOVA table).
- Right-click and choose **Copy**.
- Go back to *GQtest.xls* and **Paste** the value into cell B7.

Note: Always place the larger of the estimated variances in the numerator of the formula for the GQ test statistic!

- Copy cell D13 from the *reg2* worksheet to cell B6 of *GQtest.xls*.
- Fill in the remaining Data Input for the Goldfeld-Quandt test. T1 and T2 both equal 20, K=2, and Alpha should be .05, for testing at the 5% level.

The resulting template is

	A	B
1	Goldfeld-Quandt Test for Equal Variances	
2	**Data Input**	
3	T1	20
4	T2	20
5	K	2
6	SigmaHatSquared1	2285.939375
7	SigmaHatSquared2	682.4553674
8	Alpha	0.05
9	**Computed Values**	
10	df-numerator	18
11	df-denominator	18
12	GQ	3.34958077
13	One-Tailed Test: Right Critical Value	2.217198869
14	Decision	Reject Ho
15	p-value	0.006971221
16	Two-Tailed Test: Right Critical Value	2.595598403
17	Decision	Reject Ho
18	p-value	0.00348561

We reject the null hypothesis and conclude that heteroskedasticity IS present. If we assume proportional hetero, we would proceed as in section 11.3. If we couldn't assume any particular form of the heteroskedasticity, then we should at least calculate White's standard errors and report the corrected *t*-stats and confidence intervals.

11.5 A Sample with a Heteroskedastic Partition

In the model of food expenditures, it seems reasonable to assume a particular form of the heteroskedasticity; that is, proportional to income. In some models, another form of heteroskedasticity may be appropriate, called a *heteroskedastic partition*. For example, with time-series data, perhaps an event occurs which causes the model variance to change, so that part of the data has one (constant) variance, and the other part has another (constant) variance. In this case, there is a way to transform the heteroskedastic data into homoskedastic data and perform generalized least squares estimation as we did in section 11.3.

11.5.1 Generalized Least Squares Estimation of the Supply of Wheat

To illustrate a model with a heteroskedastic partition, we use a model of wheat supply as a function of its price, technology, and weather. To proxy changes in technology, we use a simple time-trend variable for the 26 years of data that we have. Since there is no available proxy for weather, its effects will be contained in the error term. So, the supply model is

$$q_t = \beta_1 + \beta_2 p_t + \beta_3 t + e_t$$

We have some nonsample information concerning the variance of this model. After the 13th year, a new variety of wheat was introduced whose yields were less susceptible to weather conditions. The average yields did not change, but the variance of the yields in the second 13 years is smaller. So, we have two "partitions", each with its own variance. The two "partitioned" models are

$$q_t = \beta_1 + \beta_2 p_t + \beta_3 t + e_t \quad \text{and var}(e_t) = \sigma_1^2 \text{ for } t=1, 2, ..., 13$$

$$q_t = \beta_1 + \beta_2 p_t + \beta_3 t + e_t \quad \text{and var}(e_t) = \sigma_2^2 \text{ for } t=14, 15, ..., 26$$

In order to obtain a homoskedastic model, we will transform the data by using the estimated variances from each partition. We divide the data on the first 13 observations by the estimated variance from a regression using just those observations, and divide the last 13 observations by the estimated variance obtained from the regression using just these data. Then we "pool" the transformed data and perform generalized least squares estimation to obtain the correct estimates.

- Open the data file named *table11-1.dat* and immediately **Save As** *wheat.xls*.
- Choose **Insert/Rows** to place a new row at the top of the worksheet.
- Label columns A, B, and C *q*, *p*, and *t* respectively.
- Run a regression, using cells A2 through A14 as the **Y-Range**, and cells B2 through C14 as the **X-Range**.
- Do **NOT** include labels.
- Place the output on the worksheet named *part1*.

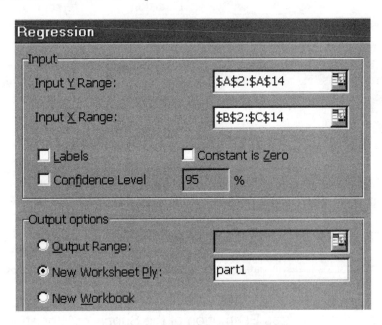

- Run a second regression, using cells A15 through A27 as the **Y-Range**, and cells B15 through C27 as the **X-Range**.
- Do **NOT** include labels.
- Place the output on the worksheet named *part2*.

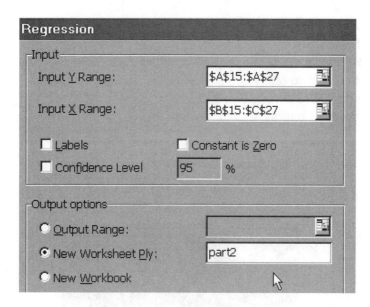

The estimated variances of the models are what we are interested in; no other output from the regressions is important at this point. Now, we'll transform the data by dividing by the appropriate estimated variance.

- The simplest thing to do at this point is to **simply write down** the values of the MS Residuals from the ANOVA tables of the regressions. From *part1*, the value is 641.6407; from *part2*, it is 57.75855.
- Label columns D, E, F, and G, respectively, *y**, *int**, *p**, and *t**.
- In cell D2, type **=A2/641.6407**.
- Copy this formula down the column.
- In cell E2, type **=1/641.6407**.
- In cell F2, type **=B2/641.6407**.
- Copy the formula in cell F2 to cell G2.
- Highlight cells E2 through G2.
- Copy the formulas down to row 14, inclusive.

	=1/641.6407			
C	D	E	F	G
	q*	int*	p*	t*
1	0.307961	0.001559	0.002291	0.001559
2	0.218346	0.001559	0.002026	0.003117
3	0.252945	0.001559	0.002478	0.004676
4	0.259491	0.001559	0.002244	0.006234
5	0.248581	0.001559	0.002946	0.007793
6	0.304844	0.001559	0.002322	0.009351
7	0.32261	0.001559	0.003023	0.01091
8	0.340377	0.001559	0.002369	0.012468
9	0.372483	0.001559	0.003351	0.014027
10	0.324481	0.001559	0.003257	0.015585
11	0.394925	0.001559	0.002712	0.017144
12	0.434355	0.001559	0.003912	0.018702
13	0.344585	0.001559	0.003335	0.020261
14	4.155229			

- In cell D15, type =**A15/57.75855**.
- In cell E15, type =**1/57.75855**.
- In cell F15, type =**B15/57.75855**.
- Copy the formula in cell F15 to cell G15.
- Highlight cells D15 through G15.
- Copy the formulas down the remainder of the columns.

	=A15/57.75855			
C	D	E	F	G
11	0.394925	0.001559	0.002712	0.017144
12	0.434355	0.001559	0.003912	0.018702
13	0.344585	0.001559	0.003335	0.020261
14	4.155229	0.017313	0.041899	0.242388
15	4.087706	0.017313	0.042418	0.259702
16	4.060005	0.017313	0.042245	0.277015
17	4.137916	0.017313	0.039128	0.294329
18	4.473797	0.017313	0.043284	0.311642
19	4.292005	0.017313	0.041725	0.328956
20	4.712722	0.017313	0.048997	0.346269
21	4.608841	0.017313	0.048305	0.363583
22	4.918752	0.017313	0.054884	0.380896
23	4.906633	0.017313	0.048997	0.398209
24	4.802752	0.017313	0.046573	0.415523
25	5.21135	0.017313	0.063194	0.432836
26	4.872006	0.017313	0.058173	0.45015

- Run a regression, using $q*$ as the **Y-Range** and $int*$, $p*$, and $t*$ as the **X-Range**. Include all 26 observations!
- Include labels and check the **Labels** box.
- Suppress the intercept by checking the **Constant is Zero** box.
- Save the output to a worksheet named *glsreg*.
- Click **OK**.

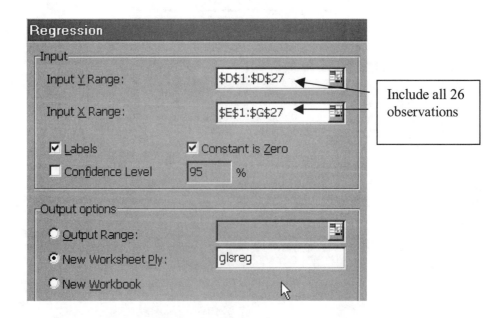

A portion of the regression output is

Standard Error	0.091937781			
Observations	26			
ANOVA				
	df	SS	MS	F
Regression	3	118.4290518	39.47635061	4670.344955
Residual	23	0.19440878	0.008452556	
Total	26	118.6234606		
	Coefficients	Standard Error	t Stat	P-value
Intercept	0	#N/A	#N/A	#N/A
int*	137.3995907	10.02731474	13.70253097	1.49853E-12
p*	22.03703829	6.443979854	3.419786963	0.002343354
t*	3.257310051	0.673827366	4.834042387	7.0428E-05

These values are slightly different from those in *UE/2* because we have divided by a less rounded scaling factor when transforming the data. The interpretations for the marginal effects are as usual. An increase in the price by one unit increases the supply of wheat by 22.4 units. For each year that passes, technology increases the supply of wheat by 3.26 units (holding price constant). The standard errors are smaller enough so that the parameters β_2 and β_3 are statistically different from zero. However, the 95% confidence intervals are somewhat wide.

11.5.2 Testing the Variance Assumption

Now that we've gone through all the trouble of transforming our data and performing generalized least squares, let's test to see whether this form of heteroskedasticity is actually present. We plot the residuals against time, since we're assuming that the variance changed after the 13th year. Then we'll use the Goldfeld-Quandt test template that we created in section 11.4.2.

- Return to the worksheet containing the original data.
- Run a (regular OLS) regression, using all 27 observations. Use *q* as the **Y-Range** and *p* and *t* as the **X-Range**.
- Include labels and check the **Labels** box.
- Choose the **Residuals** option.
- Place on a worksheet named *noglsreg*.
- Click **OK**.

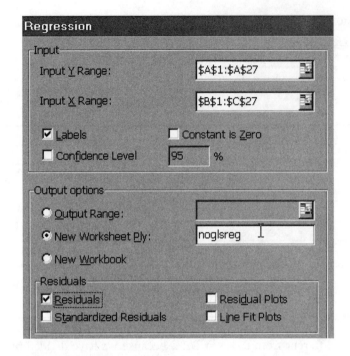

- Return to the worksheet containing the original data.
- **Copy** cells C1 to C27, which contain the original variable *t* to column A of a new worksheet named *residsplot*. (Insert a new worksheet and name it).
- Return to *noglsreg* and **Copy** cells C25 to C51, which contain the estimated error terms to column B on the worksheet *residsplot*.
- Highlight cells A1 through B27.
- Click on the Chart Wizard ▥ or choose **Insert/Chart** from the menu bar.
- Choose **XY (Scatter)** as the Chart Type.
- The default Chart sub-type: is appropriate.
- Click **Next**.
- Format the chart as desired, working through the dialog boxes. Formatting can always be done later, also.

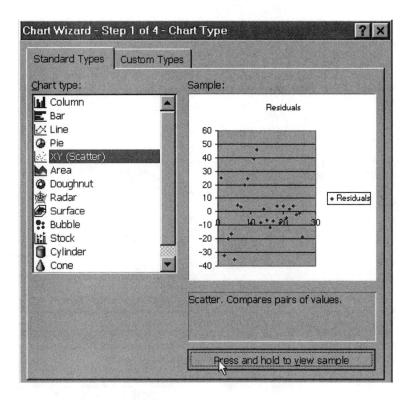

The graph (hopefully) looks something like

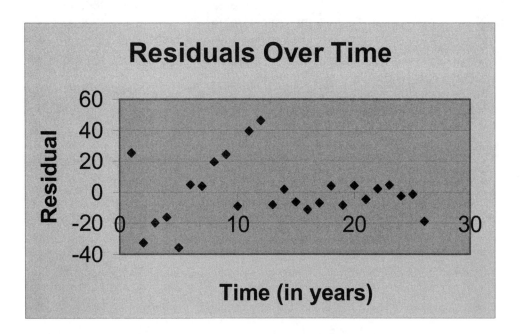

As we suspected, after year 13, the data points are much more clustered around zero. There appears to be a clear difference in the variances for the first 13 years versus the second 13 years.

Now, let's formally test this suspicion, using our Goldfeld-Quandt test template. The null hypothesis is H_0: $\sigma_1^2 = \sigma_2^2$ and the alternative is H_1: $\sigma_2^2 < \sigma_1^2$.

- Open the file *GQtest.xls*
- Fill in the necessary Data Input. *T1=T2*=13, and *K*=3.
- Use the values of the estimated model variances from the two partitions. (Hopefully, you wrote them down.)

The GQ results are

	A	B
1	Goldfeld-Quandt Test for Equal Variances	
2	**Data Input**	
3	T1	13
4	T2	13
5	K	3
6	SigmaHatSquared1	641.6407
7	SigmaHatSquared2	57.75855
8	Alpha	0.05
9	**Computed Values**	
10	df-numerator	10
11	df-denominator	10
12	GQ	11.10901676
13	One-Tailed Test: Right Critical Value	2.978239877
14	Decision	Reject Ho
15	p-value	0.000364227
16	Two-Tailed Test: Right Critical Value	3.716792207
17	Decision	Reject Ho
18	p-value	0.000182114

We conclude that the variance of wheat supply is indeed lower after the new variety is introduced, and the generalized least squares method is appropriate.

Chapter 12 Autocorrelation

In the last chapter, we relaxed the assumption of constant variance and saw the consequences of not correcting for heteroskedasticity. In this chapter, we relax another of our assumptions, that the error terms are uncorrelated. When **autocorrelation** exists, we have the same problems that result when heteroskedasticity is present. With the presence of correlated error terms, the standard errors reported for our least squares estimators are incorrect, and therefore, the associated t-statistics, p-values, and confidence intervals are incorrect.

In this chapter, we will once again apply generalized least squares estimation to obtain more efficient estimation of the parameters. We will also present two tests for identifying autocorrelation; the Durbin-Watson bounds test and the Lagrange Multiplier test. Finally, we consider the problem of forecasting (or predicting) when autocorrelation is present.

12.1 The Nature of the Problem

Up until now, we have been assuming the error term in our regression model has certain properties. Specifically, we assume the mean of the true error term is zero, the variance of the error is constant (an assumption we dropped in the last chapter), and that no one error term is correlated to another. Specifically, we assume $\text{cov}(e_t, e_s) = 0$ for $t \neq s$. This is the assumption we will relax in this chapter.

Especially with times-series data, where the observations follow a natural ordering through time, there is a possibility that successive errors are correlated with each other. Shocks to a model may take time to work out and effects may carry over to successive time periods. The result is that the error term in period t can affect the error term in period $t+1$, or $t+2$, and so on. Somehow, we must take these lasting effects into account.

12.1.1 An Area Response Model

The model we will use to examine this issue of autocorrelation is a supply response for an agriculture crop, sugar cane. The area planted, in acres, depends on the price of the crop; the higher the price of the crop, the more area the farmer plants. The data are 34 annual observations on area and price, and we will use the log-log (constant elasticity) specification to estimate the parameters. The model is

$$\ln(A_t) = \beta_1 + \beta_2 \ln(P_t) + e_t$$

12.1.2 Least Squares Estimation

- Open the data file named *table12-1.dat*. **Save As** an Excel workbook named *sugarcane.xls*.
- **Insert** a row at the top of the data and place the labels A and P in columns A and B respectively.
- Label columns C and D *lnA* and *lnP*.
- In cell C2, type **=ln(A2)**. Copy this formula to cell D2.
- Highlight cells C2 and D2, and copy the formulas down the columns.

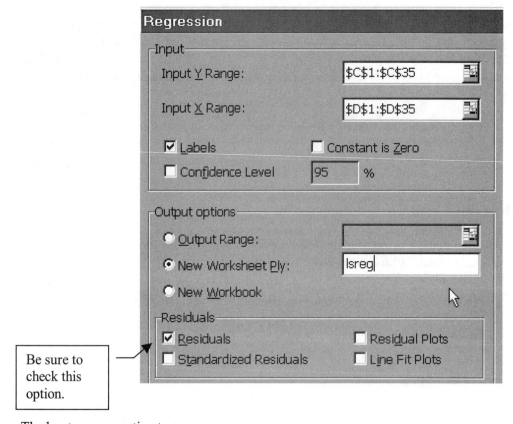

- Run a regression, using *lnA* as the **Y-Range** and *lnP* as the **X-Range**.
- Include labels, etc.
- Check the **Residuals** option so that the estimated errors are produced.
- Click **OK**.

The least squares estimates are

16		Coefficients	Standard Error	t Stat	P-value
17	Intercept	6.111328396	0.168569921	36.25396726	1.4681E-27
18	lnP	0.970582328	0.11062865	8.773336093	5.03148E-10

Since we are using times-series data, we should explore the possibility of autocorrelation. Let's plot the residuals against time and see if we can detect a problem.

- Return the to worksheet containing the original data.
- Label cell E1 *t*, for time.
- Type "1" in cell E2. Type "2" in cell E3.
- Highlight cells E2 and E3. Place cursor on the lower right hand corner of the highlighted area until the it turns into a cross-hatch. Left-click and drag down the column to fill in the values in ascending order.

=	1		
C	**D**	**E**	
lnA	lnP	t	
3.367296	-2.58683	1	
4.26268	-2.16375	2	
3.73767	-2.29189		
4.49981	-2.20447		4
4.276666	-2.21126		
4.043051	-2.02128		
3.78419	-1.95346		
4.110874	-1.56275		

- Return to the worksheet containing the regression output.
- **Copy** residuals to the worksheet containing the original data and **Paste** in column F.
- Create an XY Scatter graph with *t* on the horizontal axis and *Residuals* on the vertical axis. (See chapter six for a review of charting options.)

The results hopefully look like this.

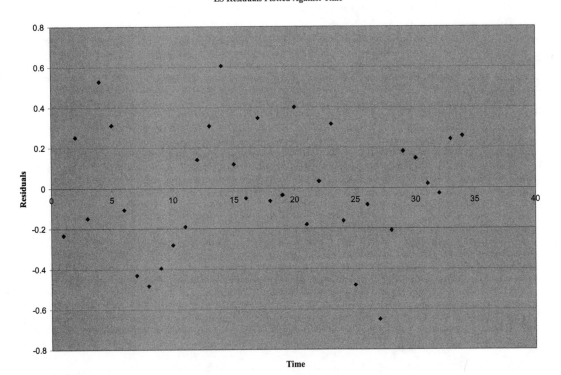

LS Residuals Plotted Against Time

Looking at the values of the residuals and at the graph above, there seems to be a tendency for negative values to follow negative values, and positive values to follow positive values. This is consistent with positive correlation between successive terms. While such a conclusion about autocorrelation is subjective, we will later look at a more formal test. For now, however, it does appear that there is a problem.

12.2 Generalized Least Squares Estimation

In chapter eleven, we transformed our data so that we could move from a heteroskedastic model to a homoskedastic. The same type of procedure can be used to correct for first order autoregressive errors (AR(1) errors depend on the error term one period before). Our objective is to transform the model

$$y_t = \beta_1 + \beta_2 x_t + e_t \text{ where } e_t = \rho e_{t-1} + v_t$$

such that the autocorrelated term e_t is replaced by the uncorrelated error term v_t. After some substitution and rearranging, the transformed model we obtain is

$$y_t - \rho y_{t-1} = \beta_1(1-\rho) + \beta_2(x_t - \rho x_{t-1}) + v_t$$

All we need to do is to redefine our dependent variable, our intercept, and our explanatory variable as above and proceed with the generalized least squares estimation. However, two issues remain: (1) Now we only have *T-1* observations since we lose the "first" one, and (2) ρ is unknown and must be estimated. We will deal with these problems, so no need to worry!

Let's deal with estimated ρ first. From equation 12.5.5 in *UE/2*, the estimator for ρ is defined as

$$\hat{\rho} = \frac{\sum_{t=2}^{T} \hat{e}_t \hat{e}_{t-1}}{\sum_{t=2}^{T} \hat{e}_{t-1}^2}$$

Since we already have our residuals from the least squares estimation, we're ready to go!

- Return to the worksheet containing the original data and the residuals.
- Label cells G1, H1, and I1 as *sum(et*et-1),ssq(et-1),* and *rhohat* respectively.
- In cell G2, type **=SUMPRODUCT(F3:F35,F2:F34)**. This corresponds to the numerator in the formula above.
- In cell H2, type **=SUMSQ(F2:F34)**. This calculates the denominator.
- Finally, in cell I2, divide G2 by H2 by typing **=G2/H2**. The result is 0.342011.

F	G	H	I	
Residuals	sum(et*et-1	ssq(et-1)	rhohat	
-0.2333	1.020655	2.984279	0.342011	
0.251444				
-0.14919				
0.528101				
0.311552				
-0.10646				

Needed for transforming the model.

Now, to deal with the issue of transforming the first observation for the transformed model, we have $y_1 = \beta_1 + x_1\beta_2 + e_1$ with an error variance of $\mathrm{var}(e_1) = \sigma_e^2 = \sigma_v^2/(1-\rho^2)$. The transformation that gets to where we want (a variance of σ_v^2) is multiplication of the terms in the model, for the first observation, by $\sqrt{1-\rho^2}$.

- Return to the original data and highlight columns C and D, containing the logs of the data.
- Choose **Edit/Copy** from the menu. More housekeeping!
- Open a new worksheet (named datastar?).
- Choose **Edit/Paste Special.**

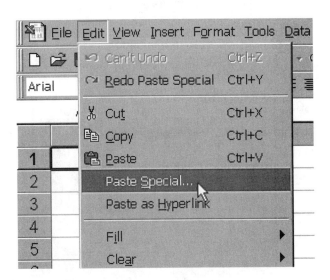

- Choose **Values** and then click **OK**.

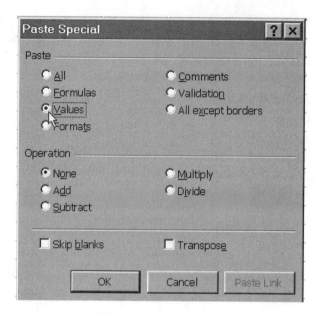

- Label columns C, D, and E as *y**, *int** and *x** respectively.
- In cell C2, type **=SQRT(1-(0.342^2))*A2**.
- In cell D2, type **=SQRT(1-(0.342^2))**.
- In cell E2, type **=SQRT(1-(0.342^2))*B2**. The first observation for the transformed model is now complete.
- In cell C3, type **=A3-(0.342*A2)**.
- In cell D3, type **=1-0.342**.
- In cell E3, type **=B3-(0.342*B2)**.
- Highlight cells C3 through E3. **Copy** the formulas down the columns.

	=	=A3-(0.342*A2)	
B	**C**	**D**	**E**
	y*	int*	x*
8683	3.164248	0.9397	-2.43085
6375	3.111065	0.658	-1.27905
9189	2.279833	0.658	-1.55189
0447	3.221527	0.658	-1.42064
1126	2.737731	0.658	-1.45734
2128	2.580431	0.658	-1.26503
5346	2.401466	0.658	-1.26218
6275	2.816681	0.658	-0.89467
6994	2.688426	0.658	-1.13548
2992	2.848229	0.658	-1.0588
8684	3.024351	0.658	-0.9294
927			

- Run a regression, using *y** as the **Y-Range** and *int** and *x** as the **X-Range.**
- Include labels as usual.

- Suppress the intercept by checking the **Constant is Zero** box.
- Place output on a new worksheet names *gls*.
- Click **OK**.

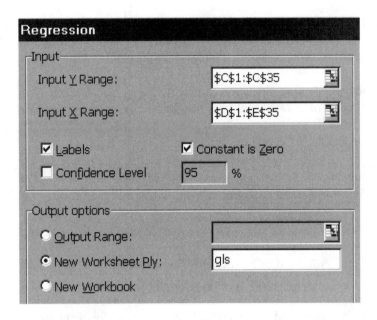

The generalized least squares results are

	Coefficients	Standard Error	t Stat	P-value	Lower 95%	Upper 95%
Intercept	0	#N/A	#N/A	#N/A	#N/A	#N/A
int*	6.164126906	0.212805425	28.96602	1.56849E-24	5.730656807	6.597597006
x*	1.006593676	0.136928435	7.351239	2.32714E-08	0.727679817	1.285507534

Once again, interpretations of the estimates are as usual. The price elasticity of sugar cane area response seems to be one.

12.3 Testing for Autocorrelation

We would like to test formally the hypothesis H_0: $\rho = 0$ versus the alternative H_1: $\rho > 0$. If ρ is zero, then no transformation is necessary and ordinary least squares estimation is adequate. Two tests are considered.

12.3.1 The Durbin-Watson Test

The Durbin-Watson test statistic uses the residuals from the least squares procedure and is closely related to $\hat{\rho}$. (See *UE/2*, section 12.6.1). The statistic is

$$d = \frac{\sum_{t=2}^{T}(\hat{e}_t - \hat{e}_{t-1})^2}{\sum_{t=1}^{T}\hat{e}_t^2}$$ which is approximately $2(1-\hat{\rho})$.

If the estimated value of ρ is zero, the Durbin-Watson test statistic equals 2. If the estimated value of ρ is one, the Durbin-Watson test statistic equals 0. Therefore, a low value of the DW test statistic suggests the null hypothesis should be rejected. But, how low is low?

The distribution of the DW test statistic is a very difficult one and depends on the values of the explanatory variable(s). Excel cannot compute the p-value associated with d, but tables are available for performing the hypothesis test, now called the *Durbin-Watson bounds test*.

Using the formula above, we find the approximate value of the Durbin-Watson statistic to be $d \cong$ 1.315979. The exact value of d can be obtained rather easily using some Excel functions. If the least squares residuals are G2:G35 in the spreadsheet, then the numerator of the DW statistic can be obtained using the Excel function **SUMXMY2**, and the denominator using **SUMSQ**.

squared diff	squared resid	DW
=SUMXMY2(G3:G35,G2:G34)	=SUMSQ(G2:G35)	=H4/I4

These formulas produce

squared diff	squared resid	DW
3.939406092	3.050865219	1.291242257

Table 5 of *UE/2* provides upper and lower critical values for d, for different values of T and K. With $T=34$ and $K=2$, the lower bound is 1.393 and the upper bound is 1.514. Since $d <$ the lower bound, we reject the null hypothesis that ρ is zero, and find evidence of positive autocorrelation.

12.3.2 The Lagrange Multiplier Test

This test for autocorrelation is based on the equation $y_t = \beta_1 + \beta_2 x_t + \rho e_{t-1} + v_t$. We replace the unobservable e_{t-1} with its estimate, $\hat{e}_{t-1}$, run a regression on this model, and then use a t-test or an F-test to test whether the coefficient on $\hat{e}_{t-1}$ is statistically significant. Since we need something to represent this term in the first observation ($t=1$), we'll just set it to zero, with no harm done in large samples.

- Return to the worksheet containing the original data, the logs of the data, and the residuals.
- Insert a new column next to *lnP*. Label this column (probably column E) *ehatt-1*.
- Type "0" in cell E2.
- In cell E3, type **=G2**, where G2 contains the first residual from the regression output.
- Copy the formula down the column.
- Run a regression, using *lnA* as the **Y-Range** and *lnP* and *ehatt-1* as the **X-Range**.
- Do **NOT** suppress the intercept.
- Send the output to a worksheet named *LM*.
- Click **OK**.

The results of interest to us is the *t*-stat and/or *p*-value associated with *ehatt-1*.

	Coefficients	Standard Error	t Stat	P-value
Intercept	6.131029548	0.161431572	37.97912306	1.45937E-27
lnP	0.982400082	0.105911628	9.275658404	1.87067E-10
ehatt-1	0.343297818	0.171173054	2.005559929	0.053699158

Recall that Excel reports a *p*-value based on a two-tailed test. We would conclude that $\rho > 0$, testing at the 5% level, but we cannot reject the null hypothesis H_0: $\rho = 0$ at the 1% level.

12.4 Prediction with Autoregressive Errors

In previous chapters, when the assumptions of the linear regression were met, the best prediction was found by using the least squares estimates. Now, the best prediction is one using the generalized least squares estimates. But now, with autocorrelation present, in order to get the best forecast of y_{T+1}, we must also include a prediction of ρe_T.

$$\hat{y}_{T+1} = \hat{\beta}_1 + \hat{\beta}_2 x_{T+1} + \hat{\rho}\tilde{e}_T$$

For ρ, we use our estimator $\hat{\rho}$. For e_T, we have $\tilde{e}_T = y_T - \hat{\beta}_1 - \hat{\beta}_2 x_T$, where $\hat{\beta}_1$ and $\hat{\beta}_2$ are the generalized least squares estimates. Using these estimates, let's predict the log of area in time $T+1$, for a sugar cane price of .4.

- In an empty cell on the worksheet containing the original data, type the formula **=C35-6.1641-(1.066*D35)**. This is the estimate of $\tilde{e}_T$. The result is 0.294713.
- In another empty cell, type the formula for the prediction of y_{T+1}. Type **=6.1641+(1.066*(LN(0.4)))+(0.342*0.295)**. The result is 5.288224.
- To get our final answer back to original units, next to this result, type **=EXP(J8)**, where J8 contains the result in the previous step. The result is 197.9915.

Chapter 13 Random Regressors and Moment Based Estimation

By now, you are intimately familiar with of the assumptions of the linear regression. In the last two chapters, we relaxed the assumption of constant variance, and then the assumption of uncorrelated error terms. We saw the problems resulting from performing least squares estimation on data that did not meet our assumptions. We also saw how to test our assumptions, and provided solutions that overcame the problems associated with heteroskedasticity and autocorrelation.

In this chapter, we once again relax one of our model assumptions, that the explanatory variable x is not random. A variable is considered random when its value is not known ahead of time, and takes on various values. As such, it certainly seems that x is random since we observe both y and x at the point of sampling.

When x is random, the relationship between x and the error term, e, is crucial in deciding whether ordinary least squares estimation is appropriate. If x and e are uncorrelated, then least squares can, and should, be used. However, if $cov(x, e) \neq 0$, then the least squares estimators are inconsistent and a different procedure, called *instrumental variable (IV) estimation*, should be used. Sometimes called *two-stage least squares estimation*, IV is not directly available in Excel as a built-in function. But we will see in this chapter how easy it is to perform IV estimation using Excel functions you are already familiar with. We will formally test whether ordinary least squares is adequate, or whether IV estimation should be used, based on the "Hausman Test".

13.1 Measurement Errors in Regression Equations

One way that correlation between the explanatory variable and the error term occurs is when the explanatory variable is measured with error. This is called the *errors-in-variables* problem. The example we will use to illustrate this type of problem is a model of personal saving based on a person's "permanent" income. The actual model would be

$$Savings = \beta_1 + \beta_2 perminc_t + v_t$$

The problem is that permanent income is difficult, if not impossible, to observe. Instead, we use another measure of income, current income, to proxy permanent income. We admit that current income only approximates permanent income, and is therefore *measured with error*, creating the possibility of correlation with the error term. The model we will estimate is

$$y_t = \beta_1 + \beta_2 x_t + e_t$$

where y_t is the annual savings of the tth individual and x_t is the individual's annual income. A priori, we expect β_2, the marginal propensity to save, to be positive and between zero and one.

- Open the data file named *table13-2.dat*. **Save As** an Excel workbook named *savings.xls*.
- Run a regression, using y as the **Y-Range** and x as the **X-Range**. (Convenient, isn't it?) Disregard the variable z for now.
- Choose the **Residuals** option. (For use later.)
- Place the output in a worksheet named *ols*.

- Click **OK**.

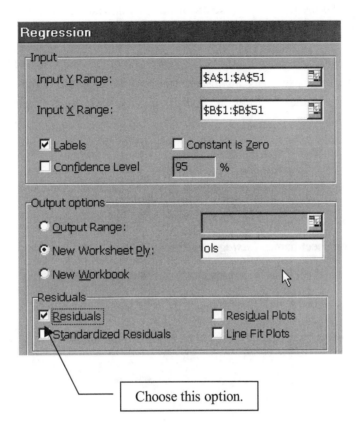

Choose this option.

The results are

ANOVA					
	df	SS	MS	F	Significance F
Regression	1	0.220741635	0.220741635	0.215796402	0.644361975
Residual	48	49.09997758	1.0229162		
Total	49	49.32071922			
	Coefficients	Standard Error	t Stat	P-value	Lower 95%
Intercept	4.342769294	0.856115677	5.072643113	6.29183E-06	2.621434365
X	-0.00518542	0.011162509	-0.464538913	0.644361975	-0.027629134

These results are disappointing, to say the least. The model is not significant. (Income is not important in explaining savings?) The estimate of the marginal propensity to save is negative, but not significantly different from zero. These results are due to a measurement error because we used an explanatory variable that is correlated to our error term. In the next section, we show how to deal with this problem.

13.2 Instrumental Variable Estimation of the Simple Regression Model

Since our problem is that the explanatory variable we are using is correlated with the error term, perhaps we can find another variable to use, which is not correlated with the error term, but is correlated with permanent income, and also with current income. That would solve our problem. This new variable is an "instrument" for permanent income, and is based on the idea that a person views permanent income as a long run average. We take the previous 10 years of income, not including current income, and calculate the average and call this z, our instrument.

Next, we run a regression to estimate $x_t = \alpha_1 + \alpha_2 z_t + error_t$ to obtain the predicted values of x_t, $\hat{x}_t$. This is the "1st stage". Then, we use $\hat{x}_t$ as an instrumental variable in the equation $y_t = \beta_1 + \beta_2 \hat{x}_t + e_t$. Estimation of this equation is the "2nd stage". You can now see why instrumental variable estimation is often called 2-stage least squares.

13.2.1 IV Estimation of the Parameters

- Return to the worksheet containing the original data.
- Run a regression, using x as the **Y-Range** and z as the **X-Range**.
- Choose the **Residuals** option to obtain $\hat{x}_t$.
- Place output on a worksheet names *1ststage*.

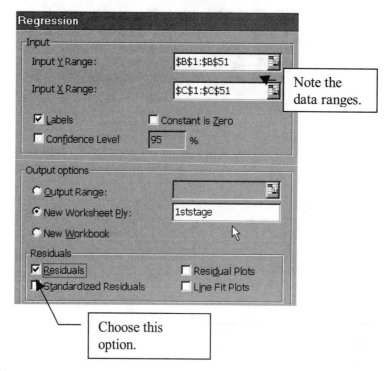

We're not really interested in the regression estimates, but rather want the "*Predicted x*" from the RESIDUAL OUTPUT.

- **Copy** cells B42 through B74 containing *Predicted x* over to the worksheet containing the original data. (Move x and z over and **Insert/Column** and **Paste** the *Predicted x* in column B).
- Now run another regression, using y as the **Y-Range** and *Predicted x* as the **X-Range**.
- Place output on a worksheet named *2ndstage*.
- No other options are needed.

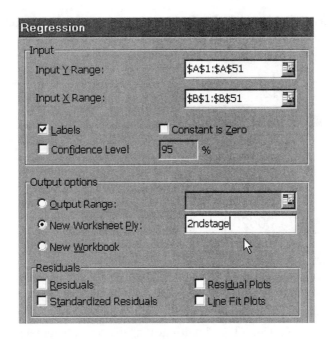

The results of this Two-Stage Least Squares Estimation are

ANOVA					
	df	SS	MS	F	Significance F
Regression	1	5.196515459	5.196515459	5.652968683	0.021457345
Residual	48	44.12420376	0.919254245		
Total	49	49.32071922			
	Coefficients	Standard Error	t Stat	P-value	Lower 95%
Intercept	0.988267487	1.253316767	0.788521716	0.434268862	-1.53169329
Predicted x	0.039175935	0.016477111	2.37759725	0.021457345	0.006046501

Unfortunately, because we estimate β_2 in two stages, the reported standard errors (and t-stats, p-values, and confidence intervals) are INCORRECT. The instrumental variable estimator, $\hat{\beta}_2$, has a variance which involves the model variance σ^2. Excel estimates this as $\sum \hat{e}_t^2 / (T-2)$. However, the estimated error term in the regression above is $y_t - \hat{\beta}_1 - \hat{\beta}_2 z_t$, whereas for the IV estimator, it should be $y_t - \hat{\beta}_1 - \hat{\beta}_2 x_t$. No problem; we can recalculate the correct standard error without too much trouble. We'll calculate the new, correct model standard error, take out the old, and substitute in the new through division, then multiplication.

13.2.2 Correct Estimation of the Standard Error

- Return to the worksheet containing the original data.
- **Insert** a new column to the right of *y*. Label this column *b1+b2x*.
- In cell B2, type **=0.9883+(0.039176*C2)**, and C2 contains the first observation on *x*. Note that the numbers come from the 2nd stage LS estimation.
- **Copy** the formula down the column.
- Label column G (the first empty column?) *num*, for numerator.
- Label column H *sigmahat2IV*, and label column I *sigmahatIV*.

- In cell G2, type **=SUMXMY2(A2:A51,B2:B51)**, which calculates the correct sum of squared errors.
- In cell H2, type **=G2/48**, where 48 is $T-K$.
- In cell I2, type **=sqrt(H2***)*. This is our correct model standard error.

=	=SQRT(H2)				
E	**F**	**G**	**H**	**I**	
	Predicted x	num	sigmahat2IV	sigmaIV	
65.917	73.19469	65.25573	1.359494478	1.165974	
64.553	70.9554				
71.658	82.61976				
64.584	71.00629				

- Return to the worksheet *2ndstage*.
- Label cell B19 *se(b2)/oldsigmahat*.
- Label cell B20 *newse(b2)*.
- In cell C19, type **=C18/B7**. (This "divides out" the incorrect sigmahat.)
- In cell C20, type **=C19*1.165974**. (This "multiplies in" the correct sigmahat.)
- In cell D20, calculate the correct *t*-stat by typing **=B18/C20**.
- In cell E20, calculate the correct *p*-value by typing **=TDIST(D20,48,2)** for a two-tailed test.

		Coefficients	Standard Error	t Stat	P-value
Intercept		0.988267487	1.253316767	0.788521716	0.434268862
Predicted x		0.039175935	0.016477111	2.37759725	0.021457345
	se(b2)/oldsigmahat	0.017185543			
	newse(b2)	0.020037896	1.955092211	0.056408523	

The correct *t*-stat and *p*-value are quite different from those reported originally by Excel. Using the IV estimator, the slope of the saving function is positive as expected, and is significant at the 5% level. (Remember that we calculated the *p*-value based on a two-tailed test). Interpretations of the estimates are as usual. For each additional $100 in permanent income, we expect people to save $3.92.

13.3 Testing for Correlation Between Explanatory Variables and the Error Term

One way to check for correlation in Excel is to simply use the CORR function. But in this case, we're looking for correlation between the observed x_t and the unobserved e_t, so this isn't an option. We want to test H_0: $cov(x, e) = 0$ against the alternative H_1: $cov(x, e) \neq 0$. If the null is true, the ordinary least squares estimators are more efficient and should be used. If the null is not true, the instrumental variables estimator is consistent and should be used.

The Hausman Test is a formal test of these hypotheses and is based on using the residuals from the 1st stage estimation in an artificial regression of y_t. We estimate the function

$$Y_t = \beta_1 + \beta_2 x_t + \delta \hat{v}_t + e_t$$

where $\hat{v}_t$ are the residuals from the 1st stage estimation of x_t as a function of z_t. (This is why you chose the **Residuals** option back in that regression).   Then we test H_0: $\delta = 0$ (no correlation between x and e) versus H_1: $\delta \neq 0$ (correlation between x and e).

- Return to the worksheet containing the 1st stage regression results, *1ststage*.
- **Copy** cells C24 through C74 which contain the *Residuals* to the worksheet containing the original data. **Move** the columns z and *Predicted x* and **Paste** the *Residuals* next to x.
- Run a regression, using y as the **Y-Range** and using x and *Residuals* as the **X-Range**.
- Place the results on a worksheet named *Hausman*.
- No other options are needed.

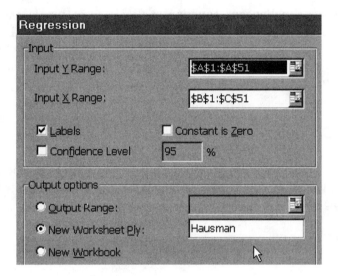

The results are

16		Coefficients	Standard Error	t Stat	P-value
17	Intercept	0.988267487	1.171676402	0.843464531	0.403241128
18	x	0.039175935	0.015403801	2.543264073	0.014332516
19	Residuals	-0.075500521	0.020095577	-3.757071512	0.000473973

Based on the *t*-test of the coefficient on Residuals, we reject the null hypothesis of no correlation between x and e, and conclude that instrumental variable estimation is the procedure in this case.

Chapter 14 Simultaneous Equations Models

So far, we have only considered models where one equation is estimated at a time. Some of the most basic analyses in economics deals with *jointly determined* relationships, which requires the consideration of two equations at one time. The well-known model of equilibrium of supply and demand is such a model.

In this chapter, we estimate **simultaneous equation** models such as supply and demand. Because the model contains more than one dependent variable, special treatment is required. Ordinary least squares estimation is not possible when we are dealing with more than one equation. (Imagine, how would you designate two columns of data for the Y-Range!?) As we saw in chapter thirteen, two-stage least squares estimation solved the problem of random regressors. The same technique can help us estimate a simultaneous equations model.

14.1 A Supply and Demand Model

To explain both price and quantity of some good, we need two equations, one for supply and one for demand. Both work together to determine price and quantity and we must deal with them *jointly*. In the simplest case, we have the **structural equations**

Demand: $q = \alpha_1 p + \alpha_2 y + e_d$
Supply: $q = \beta_1 p + e_s$

The variables p and q are endogenous variables, meaning their values are determined within the system of equations. Income, y, is an exogenous variable; we take its value as given. The equilibrium levels of price and quantity, p^* and q^* are determined by both of these equations. By setting these equations equal to each other, and solving for the endogenous variables as functions of the exogenous variables, we obtain **reduced form equations**. (See *UE/2* section 14.3)

There is no way in Excel to estimate two separate equations at one time. But we CAN use 2-stage least squares estimation as presented in chapter thirteen to estimate the parameters in the supply equation, which is an identified structural equation. See *UE/2* section 14.5 for a discussion of identification. What we will do is estimate a reduced form equation for p and obtain the predicted values of p, $\hat{p}$. This is the "1st stage". We then estimate the identified structural equation using the predicted values, $\hat{p}$. This is the "2nd stage".

14.2 Supply and Demand for Truffles

We use a model of supply and demand for truffles (Yum!) based on the following structural equations

Demand: $q_t = \alpha_1 + \alpha_2 p_t + \alpha_3 ps_t + \alpha_4 di_t + e_t^d$
Supply: $q_t = \beta_1 + \beta_2 p_t + \beta_3 pf_t + e_t^s$

where q = quantity of truffles traded at time t, in ounces

146

p = market price for truffles, in dollars per ounce
ps = market price for substitutes for truffles (another fungus?), in dollars per pound
di = per capita disposable income, in thousands of dollars
pf = price of a factor of production (hourly rental for a pig?), in dollars per hour

Setting the structural equation equal to each other and solving for the endogenous variables, the reduced form equations are

$$q_t = \pi_{11} + \pi_{21}ps_t + \pi_{31}di_t + v_{t1}$$
$$p_t = \pi_{12} + \pi_{22}ps_t + \pi_{32}di_t + \pi_{42}pf_t + v_{t2}$$

We first estimate these reduced form equations, obtain $\hat{p}$, and then estimate the structural equations using $\hat{p}$ and the other exogenous variables.

14.2.1 2-Stage Least Squares Estimation of the Parameters

- Open the data file *table14-1.dat*. **Save As** and Excel workbook named *truffles.xls*.
- Run a regression, using q as the **Y-Range**, and *ps, di* and *pf* as the **X-Range**.
- Include labels and place results on the worksheet named *qreg*.
- No other options are needed.
- Click **OK**.

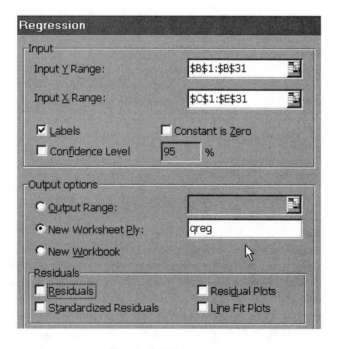

- Run another regression, using p as the **Y-Range** and *ps, di* and *pf* as the **X-Range**.
- Include labels and place results on a worksheet named *preg*.
- Choose the **Residuals** option.
- Click **OK**.

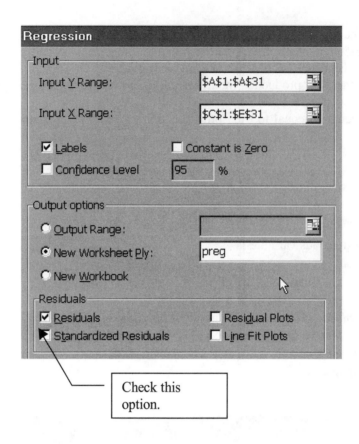

Check this
option.

The results of these two regressions are

For quantity equation:

	Coefficients	Standard Error	t Stat	P-value
Intercept	7.895099375	3.243421548	2.434188482	0.022099355
ps	0.656402058	0.142537611	4.605114764	9.53267E-05
di	0.216715558	0.070047383	3.093842297	0.004680815
pf	-0.506982316	0.121261657	-4.18089552	0.000291282

For price equation:

	Coefficients	Standard Error	t Stat	P-value
Intercept	-10.83747309	2.661411698	-4.072076898	0.000387308
ps	0.56938239	0.11696021	4.868171738	4.75902E-05
di	0.253416354	0.057477859	4.408938667	0.000159933
pf	0.451301953	0.09950208	4.535603192	0.000114522

Both models are statistically significant and all explanatory variables are significant. Now we estimate the second stage.

- Return to the worksheet containing the original data. Create an empty column in column C.
- Return to the *preg* worksheet and **Copy** cells B26 through B56 (*Predicted p*) to column C of the original data worksheet.

- Because of the way the variables are listed, run a regression of the supply structural equation. Use *q* as the **Y-Range** and *Predicted p* and *pf* as the **X-Range**.
- Include labels and place results on the worksheet named *supreg*.
- No other options are needed.
- Click **OK**.

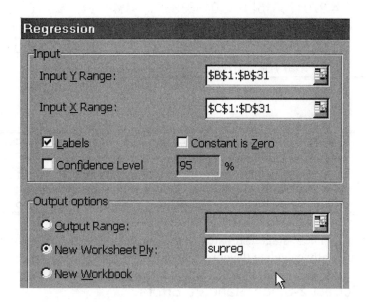

- Return to the worksheet containing the original data. Move the columns such that *Predicted p, ps*, and *di* are all next to each other. (The X-Range data must be contiguous.)
- Run a regression, using q as the **Y-Range** and *Predicted p, ps*, and *di* as the **X-Range**.
- Include labels and place results on a worksheet names *demreg*.
- No other options are needed.
- Click **OK**.

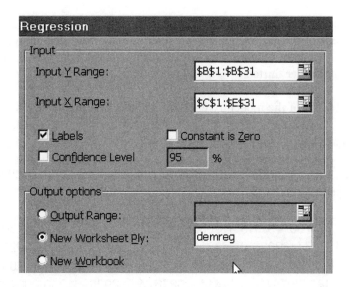

The 2nd stage regression results are

Demand:

	Coefficients	Standard Error	t Stat	P-value
Intercept	-4.279470615	3.013833821	-1.419942462	0.167504793
Predicted p	-1.123377183	0.268692958	-4.18089552	0.000291282
ps	1.296033242	0.193094434	6.711914031	4.02708E-07
di	0.501397708	0.124141439	4.038922964	0.000422353

Supply:

	Coefficients	Standard Error	t Stat	P-value
Intercept	20.03280215	2.165698522	9.250041938	7.35759E-10
Predicted p	1.013944702	0.132370854	7.659878851	3.07434E-08
pf	-1.000909375	0.146127449	-6.849564417	2.33395E-07

Are these results "correct"? The 2-stage estimates of the parameters are and can be interpreted as usual. But Excel does not automatically calculate the correct standard errors for the 2-stage process.

14.2.2 Calculating Correct 2-Stage Standard Errors

Unfortunately, because we estimate the parameters in two stages, the reported standard errors (and t-stats, p-values, and confidence intervals) are INCORRECT. The 2-stage estimators have variances which involve the model variance σ^2. Excel estimates this as $\sum \hat{e}_t^2 / (T - K)$. However, the estimated error terms in the regression above are found using *Predicted p*, whereas for the 2-stage estimator, they should use p. No problem; we can recalculate the correct standard error without too much trouble.

Follow the steps described in chapter 13, section 13.2.2 to find the correct model standard error and recalculate the standard errors for the estimates. The difference now is that we are dealing with two multivariate models instead of two simple ("one explanatory variable") models. But the procedures are the basically the same as in chapter thirteen.

(Find the correct standard error of the model by creating a column of predicted *y*'s, using the least squares estimates and the original *x*'s (not the instrument). Proceed as in chapter thirteen, remembering to divide by T-K in the formula for *sigmahat2* for each equation.)

After finding the correct demand model standard error, which is equal to 4.929966, the formulas for calculating the correct <u>Demand</u> standard errors are

Intercept	-4.279470614971	3.013833821013	-1.4199424617	0.167504793380356
Predicted p	-1.123377182826	0.268692957658	-4.1808955196	0.000291281799737555
ps	1.2960332423742	0.193094434235	6.71191403059	0.0000004027077775211
di	0.5013977078490	0.124141438767	4.03892296422	0.000422353084993566
seb2/oldsigmahat=	=C18/$B$7	=B21*4.929966	=B18/C21	=TDIST(2.27,26,2)
seb3/oldsigmahat=	=C19/$B$7	=B22*4.929966	=B19/C22	=TDIST(D22,26,2)
seb4/oldsigmahat=	=C20/$B$7	=B23*4.929966	=B20/C23	=TDIST(D23,26,2)

The final results are (not including results for $\hat{\beta}_1$, the intercept)

	Coefficients	Standard Error	t Stat	P-value
Intercept	-4.2794706	3.013833821	-1.42	0.167504793
Predicted p	-1.1233772	0.268692958	-4.18	0.000291282
ps	1.2960332	0.193094434	6.712	4.02708E-07
di	0.5013977	0.124141439	4.039	0.000422353
seb2/oldsigmahat=	0.1002554	0.494255691	-2.27	0.031731932
seb3/oldsigmahat=	0.0720479	0.355193615	3.649	0.001160096
seb4/oldsigmahat=	0.04632	0.228355864	2.196	0.037235451

For <u>Supply</u>, the correct model standard error is 1.511091 and the formulas are (not including the intercept)

	Coefficients	Standard Error	t Stat	P-value
Intercept	20.032802151842	2.1656985217439	9.2500419388	7.35758533746008E-10
Predicted p	1.0139447016698	0.1323708535613	7.6598788505	3.07433524991194E-08
pf	-1.000909374788	0.1461274489732	-6.84956441	2.33394790622693E-07
seb2/oldsigmahat=	=C18/$B$7	=B20*1.497585	=B18/C20	=TDIST(D20,27,2)
seb3/oldsigmahat=	=C19/$B$7	=B21*1.497585	=B19/C21	=TDIST(12.02116894,27,2)

The final results for <u>Supply</u> are

	Coefficients	Standard Error	t Stat	P-value
Intercept	20.0328022	2.165698522	9.25004	7.35759E-10
Predicted p	1.0139447	0.132370854	7.65988	3.07434E-08
pf	-1.0009094	0.146127449	-6.8496	2.33395E-07
seb2/oldsigmahat=	0.04991948	0.07475866	13.5629	1.43458E-13
seb3/oldsigmahat=	0.05510734	0.082527928	-12.128	2.38359E-12

Putting it all together, what do we have? Our estimated demand function is downward sloping, (thank goodness!), shifts to the right as the price of substitutes rises, and shifts to the right as income rises (truffles are a normal good). All of our coefficients are significant at the 5% level.

Our supply function is upward sloping (whew!), and shifts to the left as the price of the factor of production rises. Coefficients are significant and of the right sign.

Overall, 2-stage least squares estimation has provided us with estimates which adhere to our economic expectations. This is not always the case in econometrics, especially when samples are small.

Chapter 15 Distributed Lag Models

Things we do today are often affected by past decisions. What we have for breakfast this morning probably depends on how large a meal we had last night. Economic decisions, too, can have lasting effects, reaching into the future, often for many periods. The models we have examined so far assume that the effects of the explanatory variables are felt only during the current period, t. In this chapter, we allow changes in explanatory variables to be "distributed" over time. *Infinite distributed lag models* allow effects to exist basically forever, while *finite distributed lag models* assume the effects wear off and eventually disappear. We will deal with the latter in this chapter.

15.1 Finite Distributed Lag Models

How much a firm spends on capital during a particular period usually depends on the appropriations decisions made in the past. Appropriations are made based on expectations of future profitability, alternative investment opportunities, and the cost of capital funds. Actual capital expenditures are observed over subsequent quarters after the appropriations decision is made. A model representing this type of phenomenon would be

$$y_t = \alpha + \beta_0 x_t + \beta_1 x_{t-1} + \beta_2 x_{t-2} + \cdots + \beta_n x_{t-n} + e_t$$

where y_t is capital expenditure in quarter t and x_t is current appropriations, x_{t-1} is appropriations in the previous quarter, and so forth, all the way back to x_{t-n} which is appropriations n quarters in the past.

If we have T observations on y_t and x_t, then we only have $T - n$ complete observations since we lose observations when we create the lags. We assume all the nice assumptions of the linear regression model as usual, however, let's think about any other possible problems with this type of data. Remember what happens when the explanatory variables in a model are "related" to each other? Multicollinearity!! If x_t follows a pattern over time, x_{t-1} follows a similar pattern, which means the two are correlated. Multicollinearity can cause imprecise estimators, high standard errors, low t-stats, and wide confidence intervals. Let's see if this might be the case here. We will use a model of capital expenditures as a function of the appropriations decisions made in the previous eight quarters.

- Open the file named *table15-1.dat* and **Save As** an Excel workbook named *lagmodel.xls*.
- Label column D *xt-1*, column E *xt-2*, column F *xt-3*, and so forth through column K, which is *xt-8*.
- In cell D3, type =**C2**. Notice cell D2 is left empty. That is one "lost" observation".
- In cell E4, type =**C2**. This creates the second "lag".
- In cells F5, G6, H7, I8, J9, and K10, type =**C2**.
- Highlight cell D3. Copy the formula down the column.
- Copy the formula down each column E through K. Each column must be done separately due to the "stair-step" configuration of the data.

	A	B	C	D	E	F	G	H	I	J	K
1	t	y	x	xt-1	xt-2	xt-3	xt-4	xt-5	xt-6	xt-7	xt-8
2	1	2072	1767								
3	2	2077	2061	1767							
4	3	2078	2289	2061	1767						
5	4	2043	2047	2289	2061	1767					
6	5	2062	1856	2047	2289	2061	1767				
7	6	2067	1842	1856	2047	2289	2061	1767			
8	7	1964	1866	1842	1856	2047	2289	2061	1767		
9	8	1981	2279	1866	1842	1856	2047	2289	2061	1767	
10	9	1914	2688	2279	1866	1842	1856	2047	2289	2061	1767
11	10	1991	3264	2688	2279	1866	1842	1856	2047	2289	2061
12	11	2129	3896	3264	2688	2279	1866	1842	1856	2047	2289
13	12	2309	4014	3896	3264	2688	2279	1866	1842	1856	2047
14	13	2614	4041	4014	3896	3264	2688	2279	1866	1842	1856
15	14	2896	3710	4041	4014	3896	3264	2688	2279	1866	1842

Notice that we have "lost" nine observations.

- From the menu bar, choose **Tools/Data Analysis/Correlation**.
- Choose the cells C10 through K89 as the **Input Range**.
- Do not include labels.
- Place the results on a new worksheet named *corr*.
- Click **OK**.

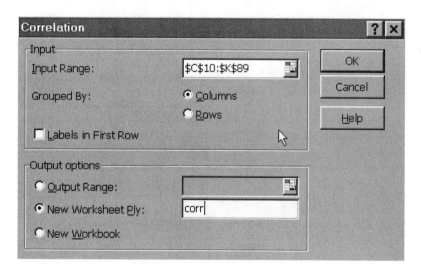

The resulting correlation matrix is

	Column 1	Column 2	Column 3	Column 4	Column 5	Column 6	Column 7	Column 8	Column 9
Col 1	1								
Col 2	0.97605	1							
Col 3	0.9584	0.98828	1						
Col 4	0.93999	0.96641	0.98606	1					
Col 5	0.90627	0.93907	0.96347	0.9857	1				
Col 6	0.86534	0.90195	0.93184	0.95968	0.9838	1			
Col 7	0.81811	0.85708	0.88802	0.92254	0.95411	0.98157	1		
Col 8	0.77334	0.80492	0.83769	0.87343	0.9128	0.94834	0.97916	1	
Col 9	0.73083	0.75676	0.78631	0.82332	0.86175	0.90499	0.94403	0.97803	1

Clearly, our explanatory variables are highly correlated. Notice that as we move back further in time, the correlation diminishes, but remains relatively high. Let's see what the consequences are when we run ordinary least squares on these data.

15.1.1 Ordinary Least Squares Estimation

- Run a regression, using y for the **Y-Range**, but only cells B10 through B89. Use x and all its lagged values for the **X-Range**, cells C10 through K89.
- Do **NOT** include labels (how would you do this anyway?)
- Place results on a worksheet named *ols*.
- No other options are needed.

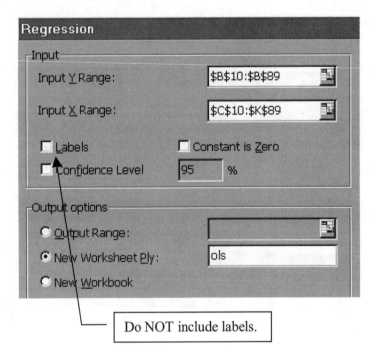

Do NOT include labels.

The ordinary least squares results are

ANOVA					
	df	SS	MS	F	Significance F
Regression	9	372314398	41368266.45	1174.767615	1.13332E-72
Residual	70	2464979.979	35213.9997		
Total	79	374779378			
	Coefficients	Standard Error	t Stat	P-value	Lower 95%
Intercept	33.41476651	53.7085821	0.622149481	0.535864877	-73.70353516
X Variable 1	0.038378825	0.034673108	1.106875841	0.272136889	-0.030774451
X Variable 2	0.067204183	0.068512897	0.98089828	0.330021007	-0.06944037
X Variable 3	0.18124298	0.089356632	2.028310327	0.046335143	0.003026942
X Variable 4	0.194434517	0.092538227	2.101126458	0.039231953	0.009872994
X Variable 5	0.16988902	0.093116995	1.824468455	0.072348859	-0.015826819
X Variable 6	0.052360411	0.091770766	0.570556544	0.570127307	-0.130670461
X Variable 7	0.052460779	0.093852713	0.558969229	0.57796665	-0.134722403
X Variable 8	0.056177707	0.094148127	0.596694904	0.552636084	-0.131594656
X Variable 9	0.127078592	0.059833555	2.123868317	0.037216326	0.007744427

The model is statistically significant based on the overall F-test, but only four of the explanatory variables are significant at the 5% level, an indication that multicollinearity is causing problems.   Also, current appropriations and appropriations one quarter previous are not significant, which doesn't seem reasonable. Appropriations seven and eight quarters back have a larger impact than those five and six quarters back. We would expect decisions further away to have less influence.

One way to combat multicollinearity is to impose restrictions on the model, and perform restricted least squares estimation. We have an idea as to the pattern of the lagged effects, that is, that they diminish over time, and we can translate this into a restriction on the model.

15.1.2 Polynomial Distributed Lags

Since we belief the lag weights diminish as we move further away from the current period, we select a second-order polynomial to represent the pattern. See *UE/2* section 15.2.4 for a discussion of this restriction. With this specification, the marginal effect of a change in x_{t-i} is

$$\beta_1 = \gamma_0 + \gamma_1 i + \gamma_2 i^2$$

When we impose restrictions on all the betas as above, the restricted model becomes

$$y_t = \alpha + \gamma_0 z_{t0} + \gamma_1 z_{t1} + \gamma_2 z_{t2} + e_t$$

where $z_{t0} = x_t + x_{t-1} + x_{t-2} + x_{t-3} + x_{t-4} + x_{t-5} + x_{t-6} + x_{t-7} + x_{t-8}$
$z_{t1} = x_{t-1} + 2x_{t-2} + 3x_{t-3} + 4x_{t-4} + 5x_{t-5} + 6x_{t-6} + 7x_{t-7} + 8x_{t-8}$
$z_{t2} = x_{t-1} + 4x_{t-2} + 9x_{t-3} + 16x_{t-4} + 25x_{t-5} + 36x_{t-6} + 49x_{t-7} + 64x_{t-8}$

We estimate this restricted model using least squares, then use the estimates to calculate the restricted least squares estimates as $\hat{\beta}_i = \hat{\gamma}_0 + \hat{\gamma}_1 i + \hat{\gamma}_2 i^2$.

- Return to the worksheet containing the original data.

- Label column L *z0*, column M *z1*, and column N *z2*.
- In cell L10, type =**C10+D10+E10+F10+G10+H10+I10+J10+K10**.
- In cell M10, type =**D10+(2*E10)+(3*F10)+(4*G10)+(5*H10)+(6*I10)+(7*J10)+(8*K10)**.
- In cell N10, type
  =**D10+(4*E10)+(9*F10)+(16*G10)+(25*H10)+(36*I10)+(49*J10)+(64*K10)**.
- Copy these formulas down the columns.

=C10+D10+E10+F10+G10+H10+I10+J10+K10				
J	K	L	M	N
1767				
2061	1767	18695	71493	403673
2289	2061	20192	74285	422227
2047	2289	22027	75928	424048
1856	2047	23752	77354	412522
1842	1856	25746	82683	425175
1866	1842	27600	91725	465951
2279	1866	29141	102747	527799
2688	2279			

- Run a regression, choosing B10 through B89 as the **Y-Range**, and L10 through N89 as the **X-Range** (the *z*'s).
- Do not include labels.
- Place results on a worksheet names *polycoeffs*.
- No other options are needed.
- Click **OK**.

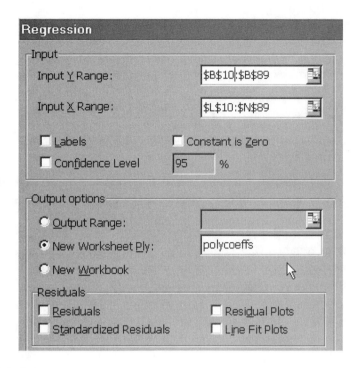

The estimated lag weights are

	Coefficients	Standard Error	t Stat	P-value
Intercept	51.57252859	53.16423893	0.970060507	0.335093497
X Variable 1	0.067167803	0.015226686	4.411189864	3.3406E-05
X Variable 2	0.038179728	0.012795303	2.98388611	0.003825583
X Variable 3	-0.005127561	0.001624648	-3.156106685	0.002292225

$\hat{\gamma}_0, \hat{\gamma}_1,$ and $\hat{\gamma}_2$

We will use these results to calculate our restricted least squares estimates and the corresponding standard errors and *t*-stats. The estimated variances of the estimators are found by using equation 2.5.8 from chapter 2 of *UE/2*.

- Insert a new worksheet into the workbook and name it *betas*.
- Label column A *i* and column B *i2*.
- In column A, type the values **1, 2, 3, 4, 5, 6, 7, 8** in cells A2 through A9.
- In cell B2, type **=A2^2**.
- Copy the formula down column B to B9.
- Label column C *b0*, column D *b1*, column E *b2*, and so on, through column K which is *b8*.
- In cell C2, type **=0.067167803+(0.038179728*\$A2)-(0.005127561*\$B2)**.
- In cell D2, type **=0.067167803+(0.038179728*\$A3)-(0.005127561*\$B3)**.
- In cell E2, type **=0.067167803+(0.038179728*\$A4)-(0.005127561*\$B4)**.
- In cell F2, type **=0.067167803+(0.038179728*\$A5)-(0.005127561*\$B5)**.
- In cell G2, type **=0.067167803+(0.038179728*\$A6)-(0.005127561*\$B6)**.
- In cell H2, type **=0.067167803+(0.038179728*\$A7)-(0.005127561*\$B7)**.
- In cell I2, type **=0.067167803+(0.038179728*\$A8)-(0.005127561*\$B8)**.
- In cell J2, type **=0.067167803+(0.038179728*\$A9)-(0.005127561*\$B9)**.

- In cell K2, type **=0.067167803+(0.038179728*$A10)-(0.005127561*$B10)**. (If you're clever, you'll find an easy way to do this!)

The restricted least squares estimates are

C	D	E	F	G	H	I	J	K
b0	b1	b2	b3	b4	b5	b6	b7	b8
0.067168	0.10022	0.123017	0.135559	0.137846	0.129877	0.111654	0.083175	0.044442

The results suggest that appropriation decisions made four quarters back have the biggest impact on current capital expenditures. The effects of decisions further away then diminish, as expected.

To calculate the variances of our estimators, note that our estimated beta's are linear combinations of the predicted γ's. Check back to equation (2.5.7) in *UE/2*. The variance of a linear combination involves the variances and covariances of the random variables involved. It is not easy to obtain covariances in Excel, so if you are estimating such a model, rely on specialized software.

Chapter 16 Regression with Time Series Data

In previous chapters dealing with time-series data, we looked at the problem of autocorrelation and learned how to deal with distributed lag models. In those chapters, we made the assumption that the time series data was **stationary**. A time series is stationary if its mean and variance are constant over time, and the covariance between two values depends only on the length of time separating them, but not on the actual times at which they are observed.

Many variables used in macroeconomics are **nonstationary** time series. The consequences of nonstationarity can be quite severe, resulting in unreliable least squares estimates and test statistics. In this chapter, we show how to test whether a times series is stationary and also whether two times series are **cointegrated**. Two series, y_t and x_t are said to be cointegrated if the error term, $e_t = y_t - \beta_1 - \beta_2 x_t$, is stationary.

16.1 Dickey-Fuller Test

Consider the autoregressive model $y_t = \rho y_{t-1} + v_t$. If $|\rho| < 1$, then the series is stationary. We can subtract y_{t-1} from each side of this equation to obtain another equation for estimation.

$$\Delta y_t = \gamma y_{t-1} + v_t$$

where $\Delta y_t = y_t - y_{t-1}$.

We test H_0: $\gamma = 1$ which corresponds to H_0: $\rho = 1$, against the alternative H_1: $\gamma < 1$ ($\rho < 1$). To test this hypothesis, we simply estimate the equation above via least squares and look at the t-stat. However, the t-stat in this case does not follow the t-distribution. So, it is now called the τ **(tau) statistic**, and is compared to specially constructed critical values. See Table 16.4 in *UE/2*. We will actually estimate the above equation three times, with and without additional terms to control for autocorrelation.

- Open the data file *fig16-2.dat*.
- Copy column E, *consumption*, to a new workbook and **Save As** *dickeyfuller.xls*.
- Label columns B through F *deltac*, *t*, *ct-1*, *deltact-1*, and *deltact-2*.
- In cell B3, type **=A3-A2**. **Copy** this formula down the column.
- In cell C2, type the value "**1**". In cell C3, type the value "**2**".
- Highlight cells C2 and C3.
- Place the cursor over the lower right hand corner until it turns into a cross-hatch.
- Left-click, hold down, and drag down the column. Consecutive whole numbers should appear.

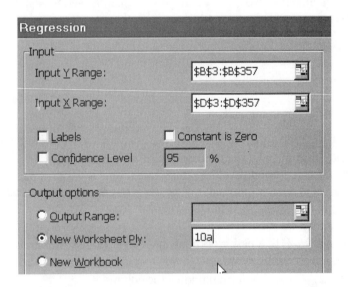

	A	B	C	D
	consumption	deltac	t	ct-1
	2179.7		1	
	2189	9.3	2	
	2178.1	-10.9		
	2180.2	2.1		
	2195.5	15.3		
	2202.9	7.4		5

- In cell D3, type =**A2**, and **Copy** the formula down the column.
- In cell E4, type =**B3**, and **Copy** the formula down the column.
- In cell F5, type =**B3**, and **Copy** the formula down the column.

Next, run three regressions.

- Run a regression, using *deltac* as the **Y-Range**, and *ct-1* as the **X-Range**. Notice that the first observations appear in Row 3.
- Do NOT include labels.
- Place results on a worksheet named *10a*.
- No other options are needed.

The results below are given in (16.4.10a) in *UE/2*.

	Coefficients	Standard Error	t Stat	P-value
Intercept	-1.514361072	4.331293482	-0.349632524	0.726822991
X Variable 1	0.003035443	0.001187064	2.557101009	0.01097237

τ-statistic

- Run another regression, using *deltac* as the **Y-Range**, *t* and *ct-1* as the **X-Range**. The first observations again appear in Row 3.
- Do NOT include labels.
- Place results on a worksheet named *10b*.
- No other options are needed.

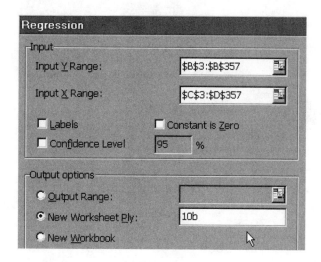

	Coefficients	Standard Error	t Stat	P-value
Intercept	2.00872411	18.88094727	0.106388948	0.915334367
X Variable 1	0.001274964	0.009259087	0.137698704	0.890557276
X Variable 2	0.015156553	0.079054967	0.191721707	0.848070748

τ-statistic

- Run one more regression, using *deltac* as the **Y-Range**, *ct-1, deltact-1,* and *deltact-2* as the **X-Range**. The first observations appear in Row 5.
- Do NOT include labels.
- Place results on a worksheet named *10c*.
- No other options are needed.

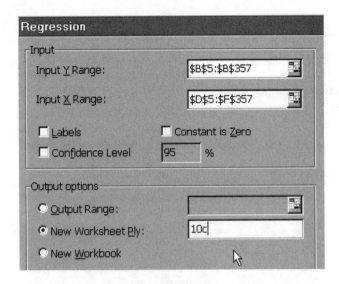

	Coefficients	Standard Error	t Stat	P-value
Intercept	-2.111455177	4.26480265	-0.495088601	0.62084913
X Variable 1	0.003965817	0.001199279	3.306833275	0.001041693
X Variable 2	-0.250278968	0.05371526	-4.659364355	4.51864E-06
X Variable 3	-0.041226195	0.053686599	-0.767904767	0.443063008

τ-statistic

The *tau* statistics are all positive, and when compared to the critical values for the Dickey-Fuller test (which are negative), we do not reject our null hypothesis, and conclude that the series is nonstationary.

What if the first difference of the series, *deltac*, is stationary? We can test this using the same type of test statistic.

- Insert a column to the right of *deltac*. Label this column (now column C) *deltadeltac*.
- In cell C4, type =**B4-B3**. **Copy** this formula down the column.
- Run regression, using *deltadeltac* as the **Y-Range**, and *deltac* as the **X-Range**. The first observations appear in Row 4.
- Check the **Constant is Zero** box to suppress the intercept
- Do NOT include labels.
- Place results on a worksheet named *11*.
- No other options are needed.

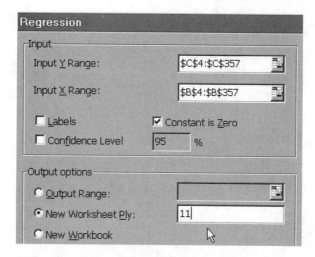

	Coefficients	Standard Error	t Stat	P-value
Intercept	0	#N/A	#N/A	#N/A
X Variable 1	-0.996948126	0.053403521	-18.66820972	1.36947E-54

τ-statistic

Now we reject the null hypothesis that this first difference series is nonstationary.

16.2 Cointegration Test

As mentioned earlier, two series, y_t and x_t are said to be cointegrated if $e_t = y_t - \beta_1 - \beta_2 x_t$. We test whether the two series are cointegrated by testing whether the errors are stationary. Since we can't observe the true errors, we use the residuals from a least squares regression, and perform a Dickey-Fuller test on the residuals.

- Return to the *fig16-2.dat* file.
- **Copy** *consumption* (column E) and *disp_income* (column B) to a new workbook and **Save As** *cointer.xls*.
- Run a regression, using *consumption* as the **Y-Range**, and *disp_income* as the **X-Range**.
- You can include labels; it doesn't matter.
- Choose the **Residuals** option.
- Place the results on a new worksheet.

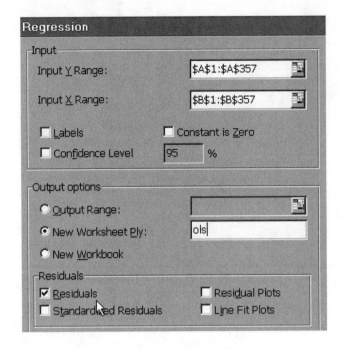

- In cell D24, type the label *delta_e*.
- In cell E24, type the label *e_t-1*.
- In cell D26, type **=C26–C25**.
- In cell E26, type **=C25**.
- **Copy** both formulas down the column.

Residuals	delta_e	e_t-1
109.7298553		
113.7466489	4.016793592	109.7298553
96.24264091	-17.50400801	113.7466489
50.69218311	-45.5504578	96.24264091
81.53700197	30.84481886	50.69218311
98.89381405	17.35681208	81.53700197
65.17537412	-33.71843993	98.89381405
65.84736426	0.671990141	65.17537412
72.17695884	6.329594577	65.84736426
71.88977523	-0.287183609	72.17695884

- Run a regression, using *delta_e* as the **Y-Range** and *e_t-1* as the **X-Range**.
- No special options are needed.

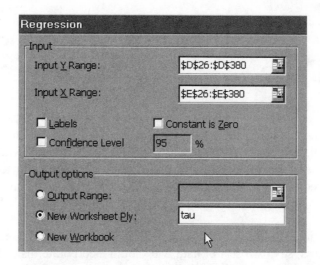

	Coefficients	Standard Error	t Stat	P-value
Intercept	0.18825004	1.699620162	0.110760065	0.911869559
X Variable 1	-0.120343702	0.026366793	-4.564214662	6.93164E-06

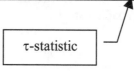

τ-statistic

These are the results in equation (16.5.3) in *UE/2*. The 1% critical value (−3.90) is less than the *tau* statistic, so we reject the null hypothesis and conclude that the residuals are stationary. We then believe that consumption expenditures and disposable income are cointegrated.

Chapter 17 Pooling Time-Series and Cross-Sectional Data

We categorize data in different ways, depending on how the data were obtained and what characteristics they have. One way to describe data is based on *when* the observations occurred and *what* the unit of observation is. **Times series** data are observations on the same unit taken over time. For example, annual GDP over a ten-year period would be time-series data. **Cross-sectional** data are observations at one point in time, over different units, such as 1990 per capita income for each of the 50 U.S. states.

In this chapter, we examine the effects of pooling time-series and cross-sectional data. If there is informational content across, say, two sets of data, we should incorporate that information to obtain better parameter estimates. The three models we will look at are (*i*) the seemingly unrelated regression model, (*ii*) a dummy variable model, and (*iii*) an error components model.

The same illustrative model will be used throughout the chapter; you've seen this model before, in chapter nine. Recall the investment function for two firms, General Electric and Westinghouse, based on the price of the firm's stock and on capital stock.

$$INV_t = \beta_1 + \beta_2 V_t + {}_3K_t + e_t$$

The data originally come the file *table9-3.dat*.

17.1 Seemingly Unrelated Regressions

As the name implies, we might assume that the investment function for GE and that for Westinghouse are unrelated. If that is true, then we simply estimate two regression functions separately. But what if there is information in one equation that could help to better estimate the other function? They may *seem* unrelated, but in fact are related. We would then want to "link" the two equations and estimate them jointly.

17.1.1 Estimating Separate Equations

- Open the data file *table9-3.dat* and **Save As** an Excel workbook named *GEWH2.xls*.
- Run a regression, using A1 through A21 as the **Y-Range** and B1 through C21 as the **X-Range**.
- Include labels.
- Place the results on a worksheet named *geols*.
- Check the **Residuals** option for later use.
- No other options are needed.
- Click **OK**.

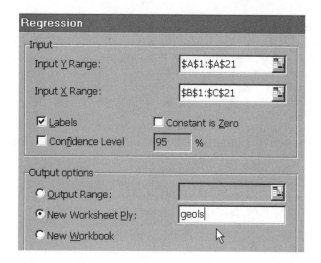

- Run another regression, using D1 through D21 as the **Y-Range** and E1 through F21 as the **X-Range**.
- Include labels.
- Place the results on a worksheet named *whols*.
- Check the **Residuals** option for later use.
- No other options are needed.
- Click **OK**.

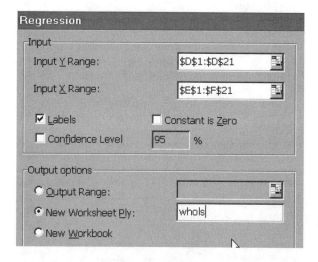

The results of these two ordinary least squares estimations are

General Electric	Coefficients	Standard Error	t Stat	P-value
Intercept	-9.956306455	31.37424914	-0.317340071	0.754849936
v_ge	0.026551189	0.015566104	1.705705484	0.106265098
k_ge	0.15169387	0.025704083	5.901547565	1.74209E-05
Westinghouse	Coefficients	Standard Error	t Stat	P-value
Intercept	-0.509390184	8.015288941	-0.063552317	0.950067995
v_we	0.052894126	0.015706501	3.367658052	0.003654762
k_we	0.092406492	0.056098974	1.647204673	0.117874323

Relying on these results means we are assuming no relationship between the two equations. One way we can "link" the equations is through the use of dummy variables and interaction variables, and then pool all 40 of the observations in a linear regression estimation. We did this back in chapter 9, section 9.2.1. We will repeat the procedure here. The full model is

$$INV_t = \beta_1 + \delta_1 Dt + \beta_2 V_t + \delta_2 (D_t V_t) + \beta_3 K_t + \delta_3 (D_t K_t) + e_t$$

In order to save our fingers, we will copy the data from the file used in chapter 9 to our new file for this chapter.

- Open the file created in chapter 9 named *GEWH_inv.xls*.
- Highlight columns A through F of the data worksheet.
- Choose **Edit/Copy** or click on the **Copy** icon.
- Return to this chapter's file, *GEWH2.xls*.
- **Insert** a new worksheet called *datawithdummies*.
- **Paste** the data on this new worksheet.

	A	B	C	D	E	F
1	i_ge	v_ge	k_ge	D	DV	DK
2	33.1	1170.6	97.8	0	0	0
3	45	2015.8	104.4	0	0	0
4	77.2	2803.3	118	0	0	0
5	44.6	2039.7	156.2	0	0	0
6	48.1	2256.2	172.6	0	0	0
7	74.4	2132.2	186.6	0	0	0
8	113	1834.1	220.9	0	0	0
9	91.9	1588	287.8	0	0	0
10	61.3	1749.4	319.9	0	0	0
11	56.8	1687.2	321.3	0	0	0
12	93.6	2007.7	319.6	0	0	0

- Now run another regression, using A1 through A41 for the **Y-Range**, and cells B1 through F41 as the **X-Range**.
- Place the results on a worksheet named *dummies1*.

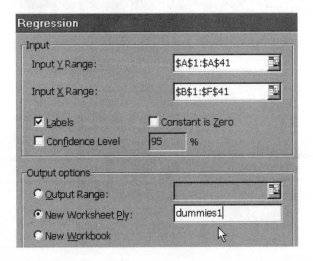

The results are

	Coefficients	Standard Error	t Stat	P-value
Intercept	-9.956306455	23.62636475	-0.421406618	0.676110524
v_ge	0.026551189	0.011722048	2.265064025	0.02999627
k_ge	0.15169387	0.019356449	7.836864688	4.01579E-09
D	9.446916271	28.80535074	0.327956995	0.744955281
DV	0.026342937	0.034352676	0.766837983	0.448470065
DK	-0.059287378	0.116946431	-0.506961843	0.61545399

From these results, we obtain two estimated regressions, one for GE and one for Westinghouse. Since D =1 for Westinghouse, we have

$$\text{GE: } INV_t = -9.9563 + .02655V_t + .15169K_t$$

$$\text{Westinghouse: } INV_t = -.5094 + .0529V_t + .0924K_t$$

The parameter estimates here are exactly as those from the separate regression equations above, but the standard errors are different. This new model treats the coefficients in the same way as before, but now assumes constant variance across all the observations. So, while "linking" our two equations through the use of dummy variables, we also need an additional "link". This additional link comes from the assumption about our error term.

17.1.2 Joint Estimation of the Equations

We will now assume that the error terms in the two equations, at the same point in time, are correlated. This is called **contemporaneous correlation**, $\text{cov}(e_{GE_t}, e_{WH_t}) = \sigma_{GE,WH}$. Adding this assumption of contemporaneous correlation provides additional information to our model and it should be incorporated.

Equations that have contemporaneous correlation are called **seemingly unrelated equations** (SUR). While most statistical packages will perform SUR estimation automatically, Excel will not. The basic procedures used in SUR are (1) estimate the two equations separately via least squares, (2) use the residuals in step (1) to obtain estimates of the variances and covariances in order to transform the data, and (3) estimate the equations jointly via generalized least squares. Unfortunately, the transformation necessary to perform the generalized least squares is beyond the scope of text.

17.1.3 Separate or Joint Estimation

When should we pool our data and use SUR and when should we simply estimate the equations separately? If the errors are not correlated, we don't have that second "link" of contemporaneous correlation and separate estimation is fine. But (as long as the values of the explanatory variables in each equation are different), there is a test to decide whether the correlation between the errors is zero or not. If a null hypothesis of zero correlation is not rejected, again, separate estimation is fine.

The test statistic we use is $\lambda = Tr^2_{GE,WH}$ which is distributed as a chi-square random variable with one degree of freedom. $r^2_{GE,WH}$ is defined as $\dfrac{\hat{\sigma}^2_{GE,WH}}{\hat{\sigma}^2_{GE} \hat{\sigma}^2_{WH}}$ and $\hat{\sigma}_{GE,WH} = \dfrac{1}{T} \sum_{t=1}^{20} \hat{e}_{GE_t} \hat{e}_{WH_t}$. To calculate the estimated correlation between the equations, we will use the residuals from the separate OLS results.

- Return to the worksheet *geols*.
- Highlight cells **C25 to C45**. Choose **Edit/Copy** or click the **Copy** icon.
- Go to the *whols* worksheet and **Paste** in cells D25 through D45.
- In cell E26, type **=C26*D26**.
- **Copy** this formula down to cell E45.

Residuals	Residuals	e*e
3.143833328	-2.860176107	-8.99191697
-0.957904138	-14.40242074	13.79613842
-3.684235868	-5.174518855	19.06414797
-7.915035651	-23.29473664	184.378671
-10.3218186	-28.03084857	289.329334
-6.613340178	-0.562215299	3.718121027
17.26483999	40.74959444	703.5352276
8.546891845	16.03552218	

- In cell E46, type **=SUM(E26:E45)**. (You may wish to place a border around this cell so you don't confuse it as a data point.)
- In cell E47, **type =E46/20**. The result is 176.4490614 and represents $\hat{\sigma}_{GE,WH}$.

Excel calculates the estimated model variance by dividing by $T–K$, but now we want to divide only by T for large-sample approximation reasons. Recall that the estimated model variance is the SSE divided by $T–K$, so we simply need to recalculate using information from the ANOVA tables of our separate regressions.

- In cell D9 of the *geols* worksheet, type **=C13/20**. The result is 660.8293885.
- In cell D9 of the *whols* worksheet, type **=C13/20**. The result is 88.66169652.
- In a blank cell, say E7 of *whols*, type
  =(176.4490614^2)/(660.8293885*88.66169652). The result is 0.531389929.
- In cell F7, **type =E7*20**.
- In cell G7, type **=CHIDIST(F7,1)**.

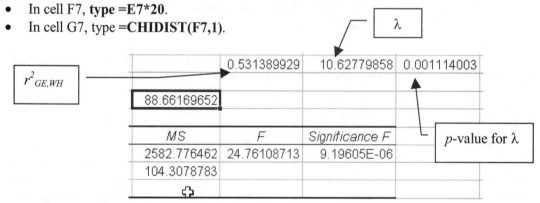

Based on the *p*-value for this test statistic, we reject the null hypothesis and assume there is contemporaneous correlation between the error terms. SUR is the appropriate analysis.

17.2 A Dummy Variable Specification

In this model, we will allow the intercept to change across firms, but not across time. Also, the slope coefficients are assumed to be the same across firms. All behavioral differences between firms and over time will be captured by the intercept. This is why the dummy variable model is sometimes called a **fixed effects model**. We also extend our model to include data on ten firms, each with twenty time-series observations.

We create nine dummy variables, one for each firm except one (the "base" firm). The coefficient for each will be the difference between the intercept for its firm and the intercept for the "base" firm (the "variable of omission"). Recall that if we include all ten dummy variables, we will have perfect multicollinearity and estimation is not possible.

17.2.1 Parameter Estimation

- Open the file named *pool.dat* and **Save As** an Excel workbook named *pool.xls*.
- Create nine dummy variables, labeled *d1* through *d9* in columns F through N.
- In cells F2 through F21, type "**1**". Type "**0**" in the remaining cells of the column.
- In cells G22 through G41, type "**1**". Type "**0**" in all other cells of the column.
- Continue in this fashion, typing "**1**" appropriately for each firm, and "**0**" otherwise. (The **Copy** function is very useful at this point.)
- Run a regression, using column C as the **Y-Range**, and columns D through N as the **X-Range**.
- Include labels.
- Place results on a worksheet named *unrestricted*.
- No other options are needed.

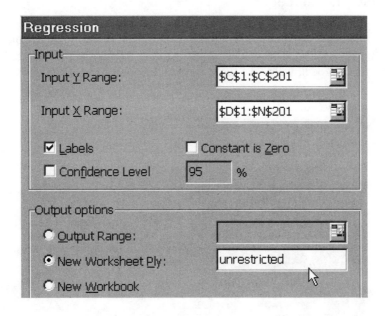

The results are

	Coefficients	Standard Error	t Stat	P-value
Intercept	-6.546268681	11.81986651	-0.553836092	0.580349147
V	0.109771107	0.0118549	9.25955593	4.70565E-17
K	0.310644119	0.017370391	17.8835424	1.98327E-42
d1	-62.59721203	50.30697132	-1.244304922	0.21493643
d2	107.4086641	26.92852224	3.988657943	9.50956E-05
d3	-228.5724755	26.49588595	-8.626715709	2.61476E-15
d4	-21.08870633	18.03866076	-1.169083815	0.243850039
d5	-108.7706342	18.42532916	-5.903321088	1.63464E-08
d6	-16.52729895	17.11168285	-0.965848835	0.33536062
d7	-60.13665757	17.43587925	-3.449017782	0.000694447
d8	-50.81232678	17.97745063	-2.826447855	0.00521589
d9	-80.7307442	17.36690142	-4.648540476	6.28015E-06

To obtain the results in Table 17.2, remember that we did not include a dummy variable for the tenth firm, so its intercept is –6.546.

For Firm 1, the intercept is the difference –6.546–62.60 = –69.146. Each firm's intercept is found by taking the difference from –6.546. Based on the *p*-values for the dummy coefficients, it appears that Firms 1, 4, and 6 do not have intercepts that differ significantly from –6.546.

17.2.2 F-test for Differing Intercepts

To test whether the intercepts are actually different, we perform a regular, old F-test, using the *ftesttemplate* we previously created. The model we estimated above is the unrestricted model, so now we just need to run the restricted model, where we force all nine intercept coefficients to be equal.

- Return to the worksheet containing the data.
- Run a regression, but only include *V* and *K* as the **X-Range**.
- Place the results on a worksheet named *restricted*.

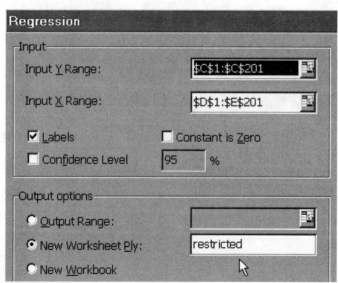

- Open the file *ftesttemplate.xls* created in chapter 8.

- Return to the *pool.xls* file.
- From the *unrestricted* worksheet, **Copy** the SS Residual in cell C13 and **Paste** it to cell B7 of ftesttemplate.xls.
- Return to the *pool.xls* file. From the *restricted* worksheet, **Copy** the SS Residual in cell C13 and **Paste** it to cell B6 of ftesttemplate.xls.
- Set the values *J=9*, *T=200*, and *K=12*.

Hypothesis Testing Using the F-Distribution	
Data Input	
J	9
T	200
K	12
SSE-Restricted	1749127.683
SSE-Unrestricted	522855.1655
Alpha	0.05
Computed Values	
df-numerator	9
df-denominator	188
F	48.99152204
Right Critical Value	1.929954863
Decision	Reject Ho
p-value	1.11131E-44

We reject the null hypothesis and conclude that at least one firm has an intercept different from the rest.

17.3 An Error Components Model

The dummy variable model treats the intercept as a fixed, unknown parameter to be estimated. We only make inferences about the firms on which we have data. The error components model assumes the intercepts are random variables, drawn from a population distribution of firm intercepts. One result of this is that the error terms from the same firm in different time periods are correlated. The error components model, therefore, is sometimes called a **random effects model**.

We know that generalized least squares estimation is appropriate when we have correlated error terms. Once again, however, the transformation of the data is beyond the scope of this text, and another statistical package should be used to estimate an error components model.

Chapter 18 Qualitative and Limited Dependent Variable Models

Since economics is a general theory of choice, many choices are of the "either-or" type. That is, we choose to buy a particular car or not, we choose one job over another, we vote either for or against a particular issue. In trying to explain these types of choices, the dependent variable is *dichotomous*, or *binary*, because we quantify the choice by assigning values such as zero and one. We then construct a statistical model that explains why particular choices are made and what factors influence those choices.

In this chapter, we examine the problems with least squares estimation in the context of binary choice models. Another type of estimation process, *maximum likelihood estimation*, is the usual method used by econometricians. Excel does not have the capabilities to perform maximum likelihood estimation, and another statistical package such as EViews or SAS should be used when dealing with binary choice models.

18.1 The Linear Probability Model

To illustrate a model with a dichotomous dependent variable, consider a problem from transportation economics. Workers can either drive to work (private transportation) or take a bus (public transportation). The dependent choice variable is defined as

$$y = \begin{cases} 1 \text{ if the individual drives to work} \\ 0 \text{ if the individual takes a bus to work} \end{cases}$$

The probability function for y, a random variable, is $f(y) = p^y (1-p)^{1-y}$, $y = 0,1$ where p is the probability that y equals 1. The expected value of y is $E(y)=p$.

We'll assume that the only factor that determines the probability of choosing one mode of transportation over the other is the difference in time to get to work between the two modes, $x=$(commuting time by bus − commuting time by car). While other factors may be important, we'll use a simple model. Assuming a linear relationship between x and p, and representing our dependent variable as fixed (systematic) and random (stochastic) parts, we have

$$y = E(y) + e = p + e = \beta_1 + \beta_2 x + e$$

This equation is called the *linear probability model*. Let's see what happens when we use least squares to estimate the linear probability model.

18.2 Least Squares Estimation of the Linear Probability Model

- Open the data file named *table18-1.dat*. **Save As** an Excel workbook named *transport.xls*.
- Run a regression, using y as the **Y-Range** and x as the **X-Range**. (How convenient!)
- Include labels.
- Check the **Residuals** option.
- Place the results on a worksheet named *ols*.

- Click **OK**.

Check this option.

The ordinary least squares results are

	Coefficients	Standard Error	t Stat	P-value
Intercept	0.484795071	0.071449411	6.785151363	1.76499E-06
X	0.007030992	0.001286164	5.466634981	2.8342E-05

Our explanatory variable is significant, suggesting that an increase of one minute in the difference between the time it takes to get to work by bus versus by car <u>increases</u> the probability of <u>driving</u> to work.

A serious problem exists with the linear probability model, apart from heteroskedasticity, which we have not treated. The fitted model, using least squares estimation, is

$$\hat{p} = .485 + .007x$$

If we look at the predicted values from the Residual Output, we see that some values are less than zero and some are greater than one. That is impossible for a valid probability function!

Observation	Predicted y	Residuals
1	0.143791976	-0.143791976
2	0.656351267	-0.656351267
3	1.066961179	-0.066961179
4	0.311832676	-0.311832676
5	0.262615735	-0.262615735
6	1.12461531	-0.12461531
7	0.851109735	0.148890265
8	-0.131822897	0.131822897
9	0.365268213	-0.365268213
10	0.122699001	-0.122699001
11	-0.152915872	0.152915872
12	0.945325024	0.054674976

These values are not possible for a probability function.

This problem arises because, in the linear probability model, we assume that increases in x have a constant effect on the probability of choosing to drive. But $0 \leq p \leq 1$, so a constant rate of increase is not possible. To overcome this problem, a model called the nonlinear *probit* model must be used. Excel, however, cannot estimate this model, and some other statistical program should be used.

Chapter 19 Writing an Empirical Research Report, and Sources of Economic Data

All of the work we've presented in previous chapters is to help you develop, estimate, and interpret economic relationships. While important (and fun!) in and of itself, economic research usually culminates in a written report. No one wants to wade through pages of Excel output; you must present your model, estimation results, and interpretations in a format readable to your audience.

In this chapter, we show tips and short-cuts on how to incorporate your Excel results into a word processing program, such as Microsoft Word. We will concentrate on the use of Word in conjunction with Excel, since these programs support OLE (Object Linking and Embedding), Microsoft's compound document architecture. However, many of the techniques shown here work with most popular word processors. We also take you to the Internet and show how easy it can be to obtain data for your research.

19.1 Integrating Excel and Word

OLE has two components, *linking* and *embedding*. Knowing when to use which is important. When you create a **link** to Excel data from Word, Word stores a set of "pointers" to the data's source. It does not store the data itself. If the source changes, the Word document containing the link changes. If, instead, you **embed** Excel data in a Word document, the document contains the data itself and it will not change unless you edit it in Word. You should embed data when you want it to become a permanent part of the document.

19.1.1 Linking to Excel Data in Word

- Start Word by either double-clicking its icon on your desktop or by choosing **Start/Programs/Microsoft Word**.

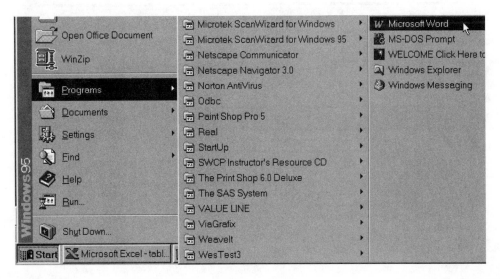

- Open a new, blank document. **Save As** *excelpractice.doc*.

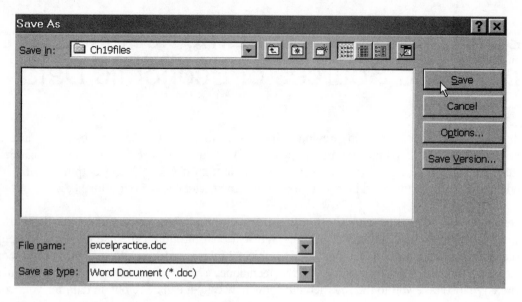

- From Excel, open the Excel file created in chapter three, *ch3.xls*.
- Go to the *Predictions* worksheet by clicking on its tab in the lower left corner.

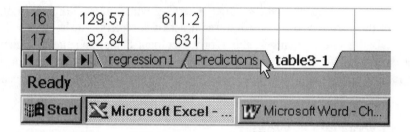

- Highlight cells A1 through B6. Choose **Edit/Copy** from the menu or choose the **Copy** icon.

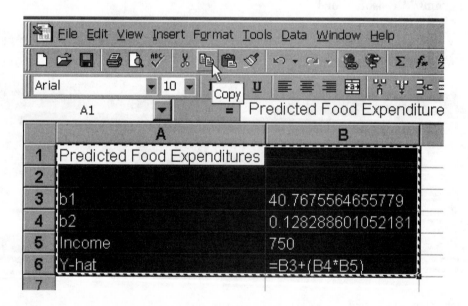

- Switch back to the Word document.
- From the menu, choose **Edit/Paste Special**.

- In the dialog box that appears, choose the **Paste link:** option.
- Choose to paste the selection **As:** Microsoft Excel Worksheet Object.
- You may choose the have the Excel object **Float over text** or not. This is your choice.
- Click OK.

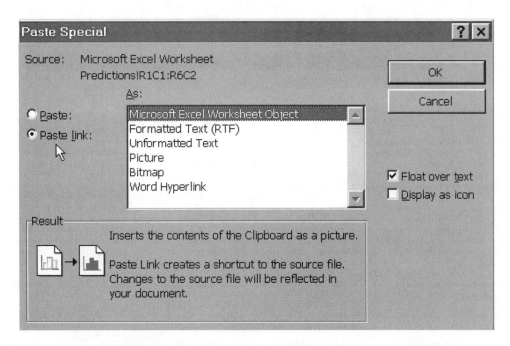

The Excel data appears as a "table" in Word. But it really isn't a table; it is an Excel *object*. Deselect the object by clicking anywhere outside the table. Select it again by clicking once on the table. When selected, the table has "handles" around it and can be moved, resized, deleted, etc.

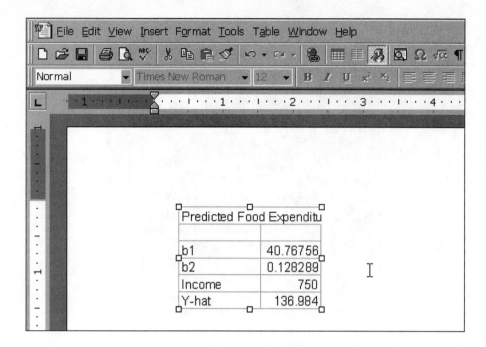

- Return to the Excel worksheet containing the source.
- Hit the Esc button on the upper left side of the keyboard to de-select the cells.
- Change the value of income in cell B5 to 900 and hit Enter.
- Switch back to the Word document and VOILA! The changes appear here!

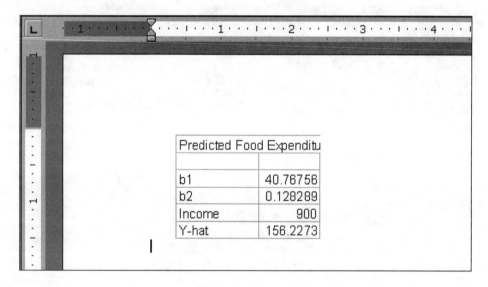

From now on, whenever changes are made in the Excel file, they will also appear in this Word document.

19.1.2 Embedding Excel Data into Word

Suppose now you want to simply report some results from Excel in Word, but you don't want the values to ever change in the document. In this case, you want to embed the data.

- Return to the *Predictions* worksheet in Excel.
- Once again, highlight cells A1 through B6.
- Choose **Edit/Copy** from the menu or click on the **Copy** icon.
- Switch over to the *excelpractice* Word document.
- Place the cursor outside the table that is already there.
- Choose **Edit/Paste** from the menu or click on the **Paste** icon.

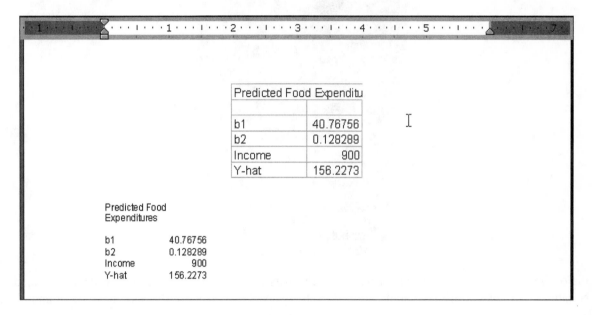

Now the results appear as a true table in Word. To clearly see this,

- Place your cursor somewhere in the table.
- Choose **Table/Show Gridlines** from the menu.

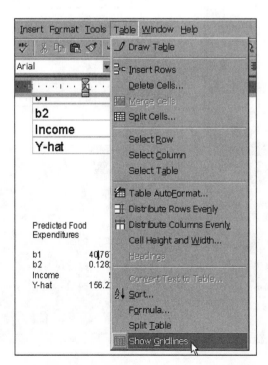

One nice feature in Word is the ability to format tables in all kinds of ways. Many predefined formats come with Word.

- From the menu, choose **Table/Table AutoFormat**.

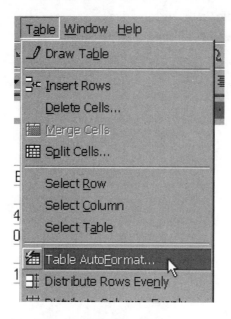

A dialog box appears. You can scroll down the Formats: and they will appear in the Preview window. You can choose what formats to apply and where to apply them. Choose the format you like and click **OK**.

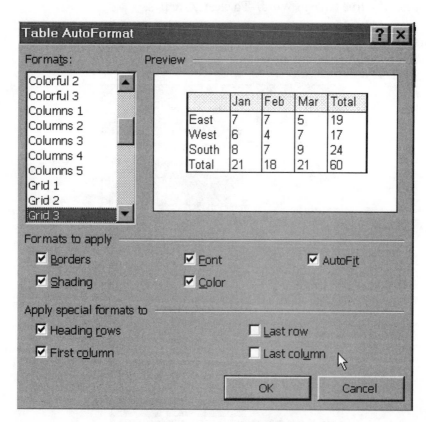

Predicted Food Expenditures	
b1	40.76756
b2	0.128289
Income	900
Y-hat	156.2273

19.2 Obtaining Economic Data from the Internet

Getting data for economic research is much easier today than it was years ago. Before the Internet, hours would be spent in libraries, looking for and copying down data by hand. Now, we have access to wonderful sources of data right at our fingertips. You are encouraged to visit the sites listed in *UE/2*, as well as doing a search from within your browser. Here, we show how to download data from two different websites.

We are interested in estimating a simple model of GDP as a function of personal consumption.

$$Y_t = \beta_1 + \beta_2 C_t + e_t$$

(Of course, we know the problems associated with this model, right?)

19.2.1 Obtaining Data from Economagic

- Open your Internet browser. (Here, we show using Netscape Communicator.)
- On the Location or Address bar, type **http://www.economagic.com**.   (Actually, the http:// is not needed.)

- Follow the instructions as shown in the next series of pictures. (Lines separate each step.)

o <u>Internal Revenue Service</u>: Tax Collections

o **Department of Commerce**
  - ■ <u>BEA: National Accounts (GDP)</u>: 137 series
  - ■ <u>BEA: Gross State Product (GSP)</u>: 120 series
  - ■ <u>BEA: State Personal Income, Per Capita, and Population</u>: 177 series
  - ■ <u>Business Cycle Indicators</u>: Not updated, but popular

o <u>Department of the Treasury: US Public Debt</u>

o **<u>Department of Energy: Monthly Energy</u>**

> Scroll down and click on this link.

Gross Domestic Product

```
Y          Gross domestic product
C      Personal consumption expenditu
           Durable goods
```

> Choose this data series.

Series Title: Gross domestic product; Billions of dollars

For this series: **Numerical Data** | **Source** | **Forecast** | **GIF Chart** | **PDF Chart** | **Exc**
Transform this series | **Display series in COPY/PASTE format**
Advanced Menu: **Save Series to Personal Workspace** | **ACF**

```
1946 01   210.6
1946 02   218.4
1946 03   228.2
```

- At this point, a new screen shows that this series has been put into your workspace. Hit the Back button on your browser until you are back to the data links. Choose the next data file.

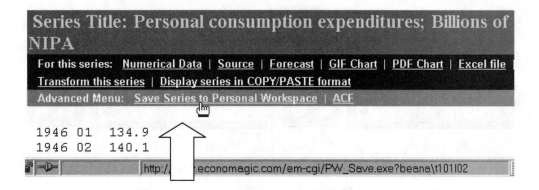

Browse NIPA Data of the Bur

Gross Domestic Product

```
Y        Gross domestic product
C     Personal consumption expenditures
            Durable goods
            Nondurable goods
            Services
```

Series Title: Personal consumption expenditures; Billions of NIPA

For this series: **Numerical Data** | **Source** | **Forecast** | **GIF Chart** | **PDF Chart** | **Excel file**
Transform this series | **Display series in COPY/PASTE format**
Advanced Menu: **Save Series to Personal Workspace** | **ACF**

```
1946 01   134.9
1946 02   140.1
```

http://...economagic.com/em-cgi/PW_Save.exe?beana\t101l02

Current Personal Workspace

If you wish, choose one or two series for transformations.

○ ○ No Series1 chosen
○ ○ No Series2 chosen
● ○ Gross domestic product; Billions of dollars SAAR; NIPA //period=quarterly
○ ● Personal consumption expenditures; Billions of dollars SAAR; NIPA //period=quarterly

Set these as Series 1 and Series 2.

Copy Multiple Series to One Excel File, or Display in Copy & Paste Format

Click here to start

Copy several series to a spreadsheet

Input Series # 1   Gross domestic product; Billions of dollars SAAR;
NIPA//period=quarterly

Input Series # 2   Personal consumption expenditures; Billions of dollars SAAR;
NIPA//period=quarterly

Change these
to "1" and "2".

Excel ⦿ Copy and Paste format ○

Use number 1 for the first series, 2 for the second etc.. Use zero to series.

Please be patient with the creation of Excel files. This could take at
seconds.

Copy selected series

Please find your 2 series in the excel file linked below.

Series #1: Gross domestic product; Billions of dollars SAAR; NIPA//period=quarterly
Series #2: Personal consumption expenditures; Billions of dollars SAAR;
NIPA//period=quarterly

Click here for your data in an Excel file

At this point, you will download the files into Excel. Depending on your browser, Excel may open automatically and the data will appear, or you may be asked to save the data to disc. In any event, the data should appear as

	A	B	C	D	E	F	G
1	http://www.economagic.com/						
2	Series #1	Gross domestic product; Billions of dollars SAAR; NIPA					
3	Series #2	Personal consumption expenditures; Billions of dollars SAAR; NIPA					
4							
5				Series #1	Series #2		
6	Jan-1946	1946	1	210.6	134.9		
7	Apr-1946	1946	2	218.4	140.1		
8	Jul-1946	1946	3	228.2	148.9		
9	Oct-1946	1946	4	232	153.1		
10	Jan-1947	1947	1	237.5	156.5		
11	Apr-1947	1947	2	240.7	160.5		
12	Jul-1947	1947	3	244.9	164		
13	Oct-1947	1947	4	254.7	168.2		
14	Jan-1948	1948	1	260.8	170.9		

(Title bar: 1440750120252 12481.xls)

You should immediately **Save As** an Excel workbook for further use.

19.2.2 Obtaining Data in Text Format

Not all websites offer options to download data in particular formats, such as Excel .xls files. But obtaining these data and importing into Excel is not difficult.

- Point your browser to http://www.csufresno.edu/Economics/econ_EDL.htm.
- Scroll down to United States and click on **productivity**.

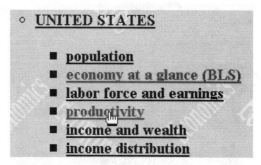

○ **UNITED STATES**

- **population**
- **economy at a glance (BLS)**
- **labor force and earnings**
- **productivity**
- **income and wealth**
- **income distribution**

- Under income and wealth, click on **per capita GDP**.

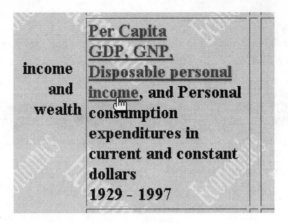

The following page appears.

```
No. 728. Selected Per Capita Income and Product Items
   in Current and Real (1992) Dollars

[In dollars. Based on Bureau of the Census estimated population incl
Forces abroad; based on quarterly averages]
-----------------------------------------------------------------
                               Current dollars
                        -----------------------------------------

                                                          Personal
                                             Disposable  consumption
                                 Gross        personal     expend-
         Year                   domestic       income       tures
                                product
-----------------------------------------------------------------
        1960                     2,913         2,008        1,838
        1961                     2,965         2,062        1,865
        1962                     3,136         2,151        1,948
        1963                     3,261         2,225        2,023
        1964                     3,455         2,384        2,144
        1965                     3,700         2,541        2,286
```

We are interested in obtaining the Gross domestic product data and the Personal consumption expenditures. You could copy and paste the data, but saving the entire file is much easier.

- From the menu, choose **File/Save As**.

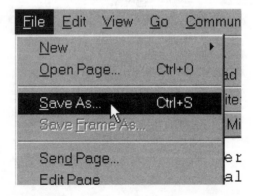

- Choose the proper folder in which to **Save in:**
- Rename the file *y_c.txt*.
- Click **OK**.

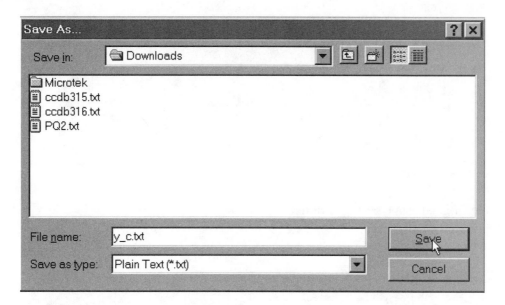

- Return to Excel.
- From the menu choose **File/Open** or click on the Open icon.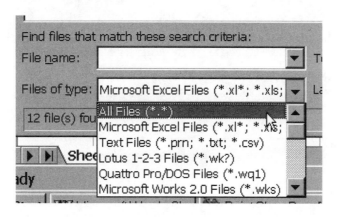
- Change the Files of type: to **All files (*.*)**.

- Locate the file you just downloaded, *y_c.txt*, click on it, and click **Open**.

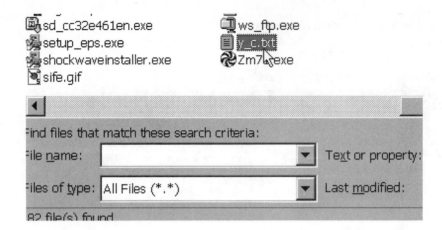

Excel's Import Wizard now starts.

- Choose the Original data type as **<u>Delimited</u>**.
- Start import at row: **10**
- Click **Next**.

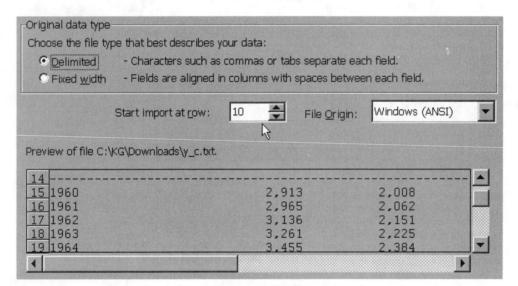

- Set the delimiter to **<u>Space</u>**.
- Click **Next**, and then **Finish**.

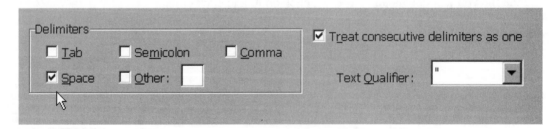

The data now appears as

	A	B	C	D	E	F	G
1		Year	Gross	Disposable	consumpti	popula-	
2		domestic	personal	expend-	tion		
3		product	income	tures	-1,000		
4							
5	--						
6	1960	2,913	2,008	1,838	180,760		
7	1961	2,965	2,062	1,865	183,742		
8	1962	3,136	2,151	1,948	186,590		
9	1963	3,261	2,225	2,023	189,300		
10	1964	3,455	2,384	2,144	191,927		
11	1965	3,700	2,541	2,286	194,347		⊕
12	1966	4,007	2,715	2,451	196,599		
13	1967	4,194	2,877	2,563	198,752		
14	1968	4,536	3,096	2,789	200,745		
15	1969	4,845	3,297	2,982	202,736		

The labels need to be fixed, but then you're ready to go!

Excel's Import Wizard can import just about any data you have. You may have to play with it a bit, cleaning up particular cells, moving labels around, or deleting strange characters, but always remember to **Save As** an Excel workbook, and **Save** often after that!